ENDORSEMENT

for *Walking Through the Valley*

"…for adult children with aging parents, seniors, and for those with elderly relatives who may be affected with a chronic, or terminal illness and are considering Hospice care. Dr. Smith captures the positive thinking essence of the emotional, inspirational and spiritual side, for improving the quality of life as a Hospice patient, living with a terminal illness."

__ Dr. Robert H. Schuller, Founding Pastor, Pastor Emeritus, the world famous Crystal Cathedral, located in California

Walking Through the Valley

ALSO BY DR. CURTIS E. SMITH

"When It's Time," - An Inspirational Work

"See, Point, and Say, Communication Guide"
- A Self-help Guide for Handicapped

"A Hospice Guide Book," – An Educational Work;
Everything you need to know about Hospice

Walking through the Valley

DIARY OF A HOSPICE CHAPLAIN

Dr. Curtis E. Smith, PhD, PsyD

WESTBOW
PRESS

WestBow Press books may be ordered through booksellers or by contacting:
WestBow Press
A Division of Thomas Nelson
1663 Liberty Drive
Bloomington, IN 47403
www.westbowpress.com
1-(866) 928-1240

Because of the dynamic nature of the Internet, any web addresses or links contained in this book may have changed since publication and may no longer be valid. The views expressed in this work are solely those of the author and do not necessarily reflect the views of the publisher, and the publisher hereby disclaims any responsibility for them.

Any people depicted in stock imagery provided by Thinkstock are models, and such images are being used for illustrative purposes only.
Certain stock imagery © Thinkstock.

ISBN: 978-1-4497-8502-4 (sc)
ISBN: 978-1-4497-8504-8 (hc)
ISBN: 978-1-4497-8503-1 (e)
Library of Congress Control Number: 2013902631

Scripture taken from the King James Version of the Bible.
Cover Illustration by Amanda Barnett, Professional Artist, Anaheim, CA
Printed in the United States of America
WestBow Press rev. date: 5/15/2013

Faith, Hope, and Love

"...the greatest of these is love". I Corinthians 13:13
Love is not love until it is given away as a gift; the gift of self.
Love is a virtue representing all of human Affection,
Compassion, and Kindness. It is the Benevolent, loyal,
and unselfish Concern for the Well-being of others.
The characteristics of love will Always guide the
purpose and mission of Hospice Care.

For all my Colleagues, Co-workers, and Friends
who unselfishly dedicate their profession and time,
to caring for terminally ill Hospice patients.

CONTENTS

PREFACE

Through the annals of history man has prayed to a *Higher Power* for healing, whether it was to Jehovah God _ as recognized in Hebrew History, commonly referred to as the Old Testament _ or an 'unknown god' as revealed in the New Testament apostolic writings.

Today, thousands of years later, man is still reaching out to God _ *as he knows him* _ for healing power in the spiritual, emotional, mental and physical sense. Indeed, history has not dimmed the prospects of those who *still believe* in a living, loving God. Medical science continues to investigate the *"healing power of prayer"* demonstrated by ongoing research studies.

Whether one *believes* it, or not, I, as a Hospice Chaplain, working with terminally ill patients for the last twenty three years, have personally observed the power of healing come through prayer; healing in all these dynamics: spiritual, emotional and mental (peace), and in the physical sense (physical healing).

When an individual is diagnosed with a terminal illness _ with three to six months to live _ they are referred to a hospice program. The modality of medical treatment moves from "curative" to "palliative." That is to say, the diagnosed disease has passed the point of no return. From a physical perspective there is no *remaining* available medical cure. Subsequently, they are then treated with palliative, comfort measures providing freedom from pain.

The hospice philosophy is to provide the terminally ill patient with the best quality of life possible, physically, emotionally, and spirituality, for whatever length of life the patient may have left.

Again, whether one wants to attribute these healings to good fortune, good luck, or *answered* prayer *from* a Higher Power, is a choice. I prefer to believe that the healings come through faith and belief in a Creator on behalf of the one who prays, or is prayed for.

In the interest of helping others to better understand the attitudes, actions and reactions of a family member, or an individual who has recently received a life-limiting, terminal illness diagnosis, these brief accounts _ of interaction between a clergyman serving in the capacity of a Hospice Chaplain and patient _ are provided herewith. With the thought that, in sharing these stories, it may help future terminally ill hospice patients, their immediate families, and loved ones to better understand and cope more appropriately through their *own* faith, hope, love and prayers to a Higher Power; *God as they know him.*

Inasmuch as the persons spoken of herein are all *"Walking Through the Valley..."* of their own personal *"shadow of death,"* the title of the book has been excerpted from the Psalm, written by David, the Psalmist of old, the 23rd. Psalm*(presented below), verse 4, as quoted in part below: KJV *"Yea, though I walk through the valley of the shadow of death, I will fear no evil: for thou art with me; thy rod and thy staff they comfort me."*

These accounts are actual experiences between terminally ill patients and a Hospice Chaplain, and are used with permission of the individual patients and/or families.

Names have been changed to protect the confidentiality and privacy of those who have shared.

The Lord is my Shepherd; I shall not want, He maketh me to lie down in green pasture: He leadeth me beside the still waters. He restoreth my soul: He leadeth me in the paths of righteousness for his name's Yea, though I walk through the valley of the shadow of death, I will fear no evil: for thou art with me; thy rod and thy staff they comfort me. Thou prepareth a table before me in the presence of mine enemies: thou anointest my head with oil; my cup runneth over. Surely goodness and mercy shall follow me all the days of my life: and I will dwell in the house of the lord forever. KJV Psalm 23

ACKNOWLEDGEMENTS

Many thanks to the patient and family contributors whose stories appear in these pages to inspire and challenge us.

A special thanks to my wife, Sandra, who listened to me read, and then personally read through each sentence of each story, and made many invaluable contributions and suggestions.

To each, thank you, and God bless you.

CHAPTER 1

The Spiritual Counselor

The dry, hot wind of an early California summer brushed against my face causing bead of perspiration to collect under the rim of my glasses and spill down my cheeks; my glasses slowly moved down the bridge of my nose. Standing on the front porch of a white, wood-frame house, I pushed the glasses back into place, rang the doorbell a second time and waited. I then thumbed through the paperwork describing the hospice patient I was scheduled to see.

I really didn't know what to expect. As a Spiritual Counselor, and member of the Hospice Team of professional caregivers, I had learned at a recent interdisciplinary team meeting that there was a need in this patient's life *beyond* the usual. Today, during the time in which I would be conducting a Spiritual Assessment, I was hoping the patient would be able to discuss his *special need* with me.

The door opened. I stared into eyes that were filled with emotional pain and a sense of helplessness, in not knowing what to do, about a soul mate that was dying. I was ushered into the home and led to a back bedroom. A window mounted air conditioner nosily labored to lower the temperature in the room where the patient lay in a hospital bed. The closed curtains cloaked the bedroom in a veil of semi-darkness. As my eyes quickly adjusted I extended my hand and introduced myself to the man I had come to see. He took my hand and expressed appreciation for my visit. His smile reinforced his words.

A look of sadness soon replaced the smile. I became a witness to the pool of pain and grief surrounding the dying patient, and the woman who shared his life. Two months earlier Alfonso had been diagnosed with colon cancer, and had been given three to six months to live. Without fully realizing it, like many other times along the journey of faith and pathway of life, I would become an implicit vessel carrying the love of God to this patient and family.

Alfonso, 87, and Yolanda, 75, had met thirty years ago after both of their first long-term marriage had failed. They fell in love and started living together. Their intent was honorable; they had planned on getting married. They became busily involved in, and intertwined with the lives of their children from previous marriages. The blended family consumed their time and energy. Their dilemma was heightened when they learned that their church would not recognize their divorce, nor would the church marry them. The intent to marry was placed on hold.

The months had slipped by; the years had turned into decades. They wanted to take care of this *unfinished* business and get married, even if they had to marry *outside* their church. Then the cancer diagnosis had been made. The disease had metastasized (spread) and exacerbated (increased in intensity) and again their marriage plan had been interfered with. Alfonso was no longer ambulatory. Incontinent of both bladder and bowel he was now bed bound. He could no longer leave the house even in a wheelchair. An application for a marriage license requires two signatures. How *could* they ever marry?

As their hospice Spiritual Counselor I felt a sense of responsibility in helping them to obtain their life-long dream. A talk with the Marriage Bureau of the Records Department of the County of Los Angeles revealed that there *was* a way. With certification from a medical doctor attesting to the disability of the groom, and his inability to come to the court house, and the physical presence of the bride at the court house, plus a Notary (which at the time I happened to be) as a witness would permit the couple to obtain a Confidential Marriage License, enabling them to be legally married.

Transportation was arranged; the Confidential Marriage License was applied for and obtained by the bride. A date was set for the wedding. Family and friends were invited. As the Spiritual Counselor officiant, the ceremony was conducted; I pronounced them husband and wife, and introduced them as *Mr. and Mrs. Alfonso and Yolanda Ramirez.*

With a lump in my throat, and a chill racing down my spine, I suddenly realized a service had been performed for Mr. and Mrs. Ramirez which completed a chapter in *their "Book of Life;"* the *final* chapter. Three days later Alfonso Ramirez passed from this life.

CHAPTER 2

Waiting for Andrew

Light streamed through the bay window overlooking the city of
Long Beach, California. The 88 year old female looked at me
from her hospital bed and gently smiled. I introduced myself as the
hospice Chaplain and reached to take her extended hand. Her voice
was strong, despite the breast cancer spreading throughout her body,
threatening her life. She told me her name was Elizabeth King. She
insisted I call her Betty. Finding my pastoral presence unassuming,
she invited me to be seated, and soon becomes comfortable with the
visit.

She has lived an interesting life, part of which she shared with
me. She began her young career as a registered nurse, and in 1941
enlisted in the Army. She told me she enlisted for two reasons: to
see the world, and to find a husband. Her first priority became a
reality when she was transferred to the Far East to practice her skill
as a military nurse. At the time of this writing the United States was
involved in a War on Terror. Subsequently, many of the pictures
being shown on television news at that time were very familiar to her.
Betty said she had been assigned duty stations in both Afghanistan
and Pakistan.

Her second priority for joining the military never materialized.
She served four years in the Army Nurses' Corp and never found
a husband. She noted that, all of the career soldiers were *too old*

for her; all the draftees and enlistees were *too young.* After being discharged from the military Betty did eventually meet her soul mate. She married Edward King and enjoyed a happily married life with a *"wonderful husband."* She told me *"I lost Ed to death from cancer only two years ago."* After the military and marriage she resumed her civilian nursing career, taking time out to become mother to an only child, a daughter Sandra, who called to check-up on her mother during the appointment visit.

Betty appeared to be coping well with the breast cancer. Although she appeared to be tiring and, was having difficulty breathing, she wanted to continue her life review.

Concluding her reminiscing about her military experience, life as a wife, nurse and working mother, she paused, lay back in bed, and closed her eyes. She continued, *"Chaplain, I've had a very full life, but I have not practiced my religion like I should have. I grew up in a Methodist church. Now I need to re-connect; I need you to pray for me.*

She again reached for my hand and said, *"I want to re-new my vows of faith in God and in Christ as my personal Savior. Please pray for me."* I asked her to repeat after me, and offered a prayer asking God to grant unto her the desires of her heart, and ended with the Our Father prayer in which she joined with me in reciting.

Not wanting to exhaust her energy, I prepared to leave. I asked her if I could see her again. *"Of course, I needed you, I still need you. Now I am just waiting for Andrew."*

She had not mentioned anyone by the name of Andrew in our conversation so I was at a disadvantage. *"Andrew? Who is Andrew?* "I asked,"

"Andrew, in the Touched by an Angel television program; Andrew, the death angel. I'm just waiting for Andrew," she said, and broke into laughter.

My puzzled look was soon replaced by a smile when she said, *"At some point in our life experience we are all waiting for Andrew."* He voice became more serious, *"Chaplain, thank you again for caring.*

Her eyes filled with tears as she shared her feeling *I'm glad you came into my life at my time of need. Please visit me again soon,"* she requested, and continued; *"Now I feel much closer to God."* So did I.

CHAPTER 3

In God's Time

I was met by the patient's son James and ushered into the home. Multiple family members surrounded the bed of Ruth Johnson a terminally ill hospice patient who was actively dying. I had been called by the Social Worker who informed me the *"patient's condition was declining rapidly,"* and that, *"the family was requesting a Chaplain."*

I introduced myself, shook a round of hands, and moved to the patient's bedside. Not really knowing the patient's level of consciousness I expected her to be semi-comatose and non-responsive. Knowing that the hearing is the last faculty we lose the ability to use, I spoke into the ear of the 77 year-old female whose eyes were closed.

"Mrs. Johnson, my name is Curtis. I'm the Chaplain." She replied in a gruff voice. *"I heard your name."* "Good," I said. And then _ since evaluating for pain is every hospice health care team member's responsibility _ I asked, *"Are you in pain; do you hurt anywhere?"*

"No," she replied.

"Now, let's get on with it" she said in the same gruff tone; her eyes remained closed.

"Would you like for me to read some Scripture?" I asked.

"Make it brief," she replied.

I read from the Psalms and then, placing my hand on her shoulder said, *"Your family is here. I'm going to say a brief prayer for you and with the family circling the bed we are going to join hands and say the Our Father prayer. Is that O.K. with you?"*

"Make it short," she growled. After reading the 23rd Psalm, prayers were said with the family holding hands while encircling her bed. Together we recited the Our Father prayer. I then said, *"Mrs. Johnson, I'm going to give you a blessing and anoint you with oil. Will that be O.K. with you?"*

"Yes. Hurry up!" she retorted.

Upon completion of the pastoral care service I said, *"Thank you, Mrs. Johnson for seeing me today. May I come see you again?"* I asked.

Suddenly, she looked at me, opening eyes that were as blue as the sky, and in one of the sweetest voices I have ever heard, said:

"Thank you, Chaplain, for coming to see me. Yes, you can come again, if I am still here."

The hidden meaning, of course was, if she was still alive.

Again closing her eyes she said, *"Thank you for reading the Bible to me and praying for me. I feel much better now."*

So did the family; with aching hearts and tear-filled eyes they expressed appreciation.

CHAPTER 4

I'm Not Ready Yet

Monday, June 29th. 7:30 A.M: I returned from vacation to learn that in my territory, a patient diagnosed with colon cancer, had been brought on service. In conferencing with the assigned R.N. Case Manager I learned the patient was now actively dying.

I conferred with the Spiritual Counselor, who, in my absence, had made the initial Contact for requesting a Spiritual Assessment appointment. He informed me that the patient *did* want to talk to a chaplain but not *at that time*; he was not ready yet.

A week had passed since the patient had been contacted. I made a value judgment to go and see him at the health care facility where he had subsequently been transferred to from his home.

After reviewing his medical chart and conferring with the charge nurse, who confirmed that he *was* "actively dying," I met Mr. Hinkle at his bed-side. He was resting and sleeping peacefully. He awakened at the sound of his name and opened his eyes. He appeared very jaundiced from the colon cancer, and was lethargic. I introduced myself and reached for his hand in greeting. He placed his limp hand in mine, and gave a weak squeeze.

He aroused to alertness as we spoke and looked intently into my eyes. I let go of his hand and sat down in a wheel-chair at the bedside. I opened the conversation by asking, *"Are you ready to talk to a chaplain?"* He replied in a raspy voice, *"Yes. Yes, Chaplain, I want to talk to you."*

"How can I help you?" I asked. *"I need to get my life right with God,"* he replied. *"What does that mean?"* I asked. *"I was part of a church once but it never meant anything to me. I want to know how God can mean something to me,"* he said. *"What was the denomination of the church you were connected with?"* I asked. *"It was protestant. Christian, I think,"* he replied.

"Would you like for me to contact a pastor of Christian church to come and see you?" I asked him. *"No,"* he said. *"I want to talk with you."* *"How can I help?"* I again asked.

"Chaplain, I know I am dying. I don't know how much time I have left. I want to know how I can prepare to meet God." His voice was weak but sounded sincere. I was trying very hard to work from Mr. Hinkle's agenda. By questioning him I was attempting to find out exactly what he wanted to do, and with which religious preference he wanted to work with. At the risk of tiring him out I needed to have this very important information in order to be able to help him reach his goal.

With the information he provided in front of me I was now ready to assist him according to the teaching and tenets of his *own* denomination of *choice*, the Christian church.

"Mr. Hinkle, would you like for me to explain the teachings of the Christian church and how they believe you connect with God?" *"Yes,"* he said, *"I'd like that."* I was privileged to explain mainline Christendom to him with regard to having a *spiritual awakening*, and *their* belief that you needed to *invite* Christ into the heart for him to become a *personal* Savior, and for him to receive God's forgiveness; for *individual*, and *personal* sin. He appeared pleased with the explanation and asked, *"How do I become a Christian?"* I explained further, that according to Biblical doctrine, and the teaching of mainline Christendom, one becomes a Christian *through* prayer by admission of sin (guilt) *to* God, and *believing* that Christ *did*, in fact, *die for the sins of all mankind*, and then, *asking forgiveness for sin*

(being sorry for – repentance), and, through prayer, inviting Christ into the heart to become a *personal* Savior.

He appeared to think about what I had said for a few minutes and then nodded his head as if he understood.

"*I don't know how to pray,*" He said, "*will you pray for me?*"

Asking him to repeat after me, I led him in what is known in the Christian church as a "sinner's prayer," wherein, each step, as outlined above, is followed. Mr. Hinkle weakly held my hand and slowly repeated the words of the prayer. "*Thank you, Chaplain, I now feel safe.*"

He closed his eyes. His hand went limp in mine. He appeared to drift into a peaceful sleep. I gently released his hand, left the room, and softly closed the door.

Tuesday, June 30th. 7:00 AM: From my voice mail message, I learned, at 4:25 A.M. Mr. Hinkle had died a peaceful death.

CHAPTER 5

How Long, Doc?

It's 10:30 A.M. on Friday morning. It was my first visit of the day. I stood at the door of a third story apartment in Los Angeles, California. After ringing the bell I heard noise of activity inside. Soon the door opened framing a middle-aged woman wearing pajamas with a robe. Her hair was rolled up in large, multi-colored curlers.

"You the Chaplain?" she asked

"Yes," I replied, and handed her one of my business cards. She said she was *"Mabel."*

She stood silent for a time, and then from the pocket of the robe she took a piece of cardboard which appeared to have been torn from a cardboard box. On the piece of cardboard she had written a message. She thrust the piece of cardboard into my face. I stepped back and read bold, block lettering, which had been penned with a black, felt-tip marker. It said: *"Don't tell him he's dying!"*

I acknowledged the message and told her, *"Don't worry. I'm just here for a visit."* She showed me into the living room of a neat, well kept, dimly lighted apartment.

As my eyes adjusted to the dim light I observed a bald-headed, elderly man sitting in an easy chair with his legs propped up on a hassock. I noticed his legs were acutely swollen and the calf on the left legs had a draining, gaping, red and angry wound. He greeted me in a loud voice.

"Come on in, Chaplain. We've been expecting you!"

"Thank you, Mr. Weeks," I said, *"it is my pleasure meeting you and the Mrs., and to visit with you today."*

We attempted to make small talk and spoke about the weather, the Angel's and Dodger's baseball teams, about the Raider's football team, etc. I observed the wife Mabel sitting on the couch next to me listening intently to every word I said. By her presence I was reminded of her message presented to me at the door.

Mr. Weeks and I appeared to gain immediate rapport. I found him to be friendly, outgoing and pleasant. We talked about his illness _ cirrhosis of the liver, alcohol related _ his nasty leg wound, and the reason for keeping it undressed and open to the air.

He stated that *"The nurse said it had a better chance of draining and healing if I left the dressing off."*

I actively listened, and let him do most of the talking. He appeared to be free from pain, comfortable and relaxed. A ballgame had just started. A college game as I recall, and he appeared to be more interested in the game than in our conversation. He seemed to be running out of things to say. Noticing his sudden anxiety I started to excuse myself. He turned down the volume on the TV, looked me in the eye and said, *"Can I ask you a question?"* *"Sure. Ask me about anything I can answer,"* I replied.

Although I am not a medical doctor, many of my patients call me Doc. *"Doc...,"* he started and then paused to start again, *"Doc, how long do you think I have to live?"*

The wife Mabel was startled by his question and said, *"Honey, we agreed not to talk..."* He interrupted her, *"Mabel, we both know I am dying. I just wanted to see if Doc... if the Chaplain had any idea, based on his experience, of how long I have to live."*

"Mr. Weeks" I said, *"although we can know averages collectively, we can never know how long, or how short a time we have to live. Even when we are strong and healthy, less when we have a terminal illness. Only God knows,"* I concluded

Yeah, I guess you're right," he acknowledged and said, *"I think I will have to talk with Him. I'm Lutheran. I hope he will hear me.*

I assured him that God *would* listen to his prayers.

"Thank you for seeing me today, Mr. and Mrs. Weeks. May I pray with you before I go?" I asked.

"Sure, go ahead," he agreed.

I prayed a brief prayer requesting God to keep him free from pain and comfortable, and to grant unto him the desires of his heart. I prayed that they would draw strength from one another.

I asked them to join hands and recite with me with me the Our Father prayer which they did.

Before leaving I asked him *"May I come back and see you another time?"*

He replied, *"Sure. Come back any time; you are welcome."*

"Thank you, I will" I promised. *"I will always call ahead to set an appointment,"* I told him.

"Please do," he replied.

A promise I was *unable* to keep. One week after my initial appointment I learned Mr. Weeks had transitioned into death.

CHAPTER 6

A Miracle Man

I was called to the home of Jose Lopez by his wife Connie. Jose had been diagnosed with a terminal illness of multiple myeloma. I rang the bell and waited. The door opened. I introduced myself. Jose extended his hand and asked me into his home.

"I'm glad you're here, Chaplain," he said.

"Thank you for inviting me, Mr. Lopez," I replied.

"Call me Jose, everybody else does," he invited, and motioned me to a seat on the sofa.

"What is your religious preference?" I asked.

"I used to be Catholic, baptized at least. Now I'm Pentecostal," he said.

I asked him to tell me about himself. He thought for a few minutes and then began to talk.

"Well, as a punk teen-ager I was a gang member where I got into crime and drugs. I got hooked on alcohol and heroin and had to steal to support my habit. I was in and out of juvenile detention. I graduated to armed robbery, was caught, convicted and did time in the big house.

After getting out I met my Connie, got married, and started to turn my life around. But I couldn't kick the habit. The harder I tried, the more I seemed to fail.

"I would be sober for a day or two and then go off on a binge of

15

drinking and running with old friends who would help me to find a fix. I couldn't seem to help myself. My wife Connie soon got pregnant. She finally told me that I better get control of my life or she would leave me. And that I would never get to see, or be with my kid. I really got scared. I had never been happier than when I was with Connie. I didn't want to lose her."

He stopped talking. I encouraged him to go on: *"Then what happened?"* I asked.

"I bet I'm boring you to death," he replied.

"No, not at all. Your story is very interesting to me," I said, again encouraging him to continue; he did.

"As I said, when Connie told me to shape up, or ship out, I really got scared and turned to my parents for help. With their assistance, I went into rehab for six weeks and came out clean and sober. In the meantime, my wife Connie had become connected to a Pentecostal church. She got me to start going and it was one of the best things I have ever done. So with the support of the church and the support of the AA program I attended I have now been clean and sober for thirty years. I couldn't have done it without the help and support of the Lord, my wife, family and the AA program.

"About ten years after our second son was born I was diagnosed with lung cancer. The doctor told me that I had three to six months to live. The church and my family started praying for me and I went into remission. This was seven years ago. I thought of myself as 'A Miracle Man.' Since then I've had regular check-ups and thought I was healed, but just this past month, I was again diagnosed with cancer. This time, multiple myeloma.

"I've put it in the hands of the Lord. If it's my time, I told him, I'm ready for him to take me home. But until then, as long as I live, I just want to help other people."

Jose stopped talking. I noticed tears spilling out of his eyes and sliding down his face. I asked him, *"May I pray with you?"* to which he agreed.

I prayed that God would continue to watch over him and his

family, that his energy and strength would be renewed, and that God would grant unto him the desires of his heart.

He thanked me for my visit and my prayers and requested that I see him again, *"Please come back and see me again, soon."*

I assured him I would, and took my leave. He appeared to be coping appropriately at the time of my leave.

I continued to visit with Jose on a regular basis. Each time I visited him he presented with a pleasant and up attitude, and each time he told me that he had put his illness outcome *"In the hands of the Lord."*

Six weeks after being admitted to the hospice program Jose's condition took a downturn. He had become lethargic, stopped eating, and had slipped into a non-responsive state.

Multiple family members were called in anticipation of his passing.

I was called by the family to come and read Scripture, say prayers, and to offer him a Commendation for the dying. Upon arriving I observed 25 to 30 family members present. Fifteen of them were sitting or standing in Jose's bedroom.

I was invited in and ushered to his bedside. It seemed as if Jose was actively dying. He appeared to have many of the symptoms related to death and dying. His breathing was shallow, he was non-responsive and had terminal bronchi (a death rattle when he breathed). I again introduced myself to the family members and told them what I was going to do. I read some Scripture from the Psalms, asked the family to join hands as I prayed. I concluded by asking the family to join in reciting the Our Father prayer.

I then blessed and anointed Jose with oil. He remained non-responsive throughout my visit. I whispered *"God be with you"* into his ear, bade the family *"peace"* and exited the home.

This all took place on Friday afternoon. From my experience I did not expect to see Jose alive again. I was wrong. He again appeared to be a "Miracle Man."

On Monday the following week he was still very much alive and was responding to family members, as well as eating. He was experiencing a burst of energy.

I was again summoned to the home, at the request of the family, for Spiritual support.

Jose had revived, was alert, oriented and verbally responsive. I sat with him for the better part of an hour. He did most of the talking; I was an active listener.

He said, *"Chaplain, I can't thank you enough for your support. In the short time I have come to know you I have grown to love you like a brother. I think of you as my pastor, and I wanted you to know that."*

I sensed that he was getting tired and I said, *"Jose, I am very touched by your words. I thank you for telling me. I respect you as a Christian man and consider it a privilege to be your friend, and am honored by your compliment."*

Tears glistened in his eyes as he reached for, and held my hand. He said, *"Please come and see me again real soon, if I'm still here."* I felt he might be having a premonition about imminent death.

I told him I would, if possible. Unfortunately, it was *not* possible; at 11:35 P.M. that same evening, Jose passed away.

CHAPTER 7

I'm A Buddhist

Aiko Cho looked up from her hospital bed, where she lay on her back, with the head of the bed elevated.

"My daughters wanted me to see you, Chaplain," she said fluently in English, *"They are Christian; I am Buddhist."*

Thus began one of the most interesting and remarkable cases of my Hospice Chaplain Ministry. Aiko, she insisted I call her by her first name, told me about how, at age 18, she had married an American soldier and came to the Unites States to live with him after the Korean War.

For the next fifty years she and her husband Clark raised four daughters, who were now married. They had four grandchildren. She related how husband Clark contracted Lung Cancer from being a three-pack-a-day smoker. He had died three years before and Aiko had moved in with her oldest daughter Diane.

Diane, recently divorced from an alcoholic husband, was facing extreme and extenuating circumstances on her own in the loss of a marriage. She was now facing another loss; the imminent loss of her mother who was dying with uterine cancer.

In private and confidential conferencing with the daughters, Diane and Claire, it was learned that they both had converted from Buddhism to Christianity. They appeared to be sincere believers in a higher power they had come to know and love known to them as God, not Buddha.

Now, despite all their own adverse circumstances, they appeared to be more concerned about their mother's *"salvation"* _ in their words _ than they were about their *own* problems.

They explained their religious Christian belief to me: They had been invited to a mainline Christian evangelical church where they related they had heard the *"good news"* about salvation.

They went on to explain how they both had *"invited Christ into their hearts and life as Savior,"* and had become *"saved."*

They were now requesting me, as a Christian Hospice Chaplain, to encourage their mother to do the same; to convert from Buddhism to Christianity.

With as much sensitivity as possible I explained to them that as a Hospice Chaplain I have to be neutral and not try to convert or influence persons to any form of religion and that, I necessarily had to work from the patient's own agenda, and that it would be inappropriate for me to try and convert her, *from* her religious preference, to *their* religious preference. I had to respectfully refuse their request.

I did, however, agree _ at my next visit _ to explain to their mother the daughter's Christian experience, that of a Spiritual Awakening, and the dynamics for their decision. And to then, let their mother ponder, and pray, *with regard to her own relationship to a Higher Power*, and to not force their mother to make a decision just to please them; the daughters. Rather, to let their mother make up her own mind as to whether or not she *wanted* to convert *from* Buddhism *to Christianity.*

Both Diane and Claire seemed pleased with my answer and told me that in the interim period they would also re-tell their mother the story about their conversion experience.

On my next visit with Aiko, at her request, I did exactly what I had told the daughters I would do. I explained about the daughter's conversion experience. With no attempt to persuade Aiko to make any kind of decision I turned the conversation in a different direction to a new subject.

Aiko was pleased with my visit and my honesty and said so. *"Chaplain, you have done more to boost my spirits than anyone else has. I appreciate your integrity and honesty in not trying to convert me. Because I respect you, and because of what my daughters have told me, I am going to give some serious thought and prayer to what my daughters suggest I do."*

"Thank you, Aiko it's my pleasure visiting with you. May I pray with you?" I asked.

"Of Course, Chaplain, by all means," she replied.

I said some prayers requesting that she would be renewed in energy and strength and that God would grant unto her the desires of her heart. I shook her hand and told her I would see her again soon.

"Please do," she said, encouraging another visit.

One week later I received a call from Aiko. She had left a message for me that she wanted to see me. I returned her call, made an appointment for that afternoon.

I arrived at the home, rang the bell several times, and finally heard a voice saying *"Come in."* I turned the knob and slowly opened the door.

Aiko was sitting on the sofa in the living room. I hardly recognized her. She appeared to have lost weight and her skin was very pale. I recognized the signs and symptoms of pain. She was perspiring heavily, and was expressing facial grimacing. I sat down next to her on the sofa, took her hand and asked where her pain was. She pointed to her left thigh just above the knee.

She took my hand and placed it on her leg over the pain area. Even through the robe I could feel the heat.

I immediately called the R.N. Case Manager and reported the pain. She informed me that she would come right over. In the meantime I helped Aiko place a cold compress on her leg to help reduce the heat and try alleviating some of the pain.

She appeared to become a little calmer with minimal relief from her pain. She again reached for my hand.

She said, *"You know, Chaplain I've been thinking and praying a lot about you shared with me about my daughters and their new Christian belief. I have come to a decision."*

She continued, *"I have asked my daughters to show me how to become a Christian. I like what they say about life after death, eternal life. I want that. I have turned to Christ and have asked him to forgive my sins and to save my soul. Chaplain, I am now a Christian Buddhist!"*

"Do your daughters know this?" I asked.

"Oh, yes," she replied.

About this time I heard the doorbell ring. Her hospice nurse had arrived. She quickly gave Aiko a pain medication treatment and taught her how to elevate her leg to reduce swelling and alleviate pain. The nurse indicated that Aiko's poor circulation had been the cause for the pain and swelling.

As I prepared to leave Aiko's oldest daughter Diane came home from running some errands and to check on her mother. I was pleased to see her and quietly asked if she knew about her mother's decision with regard to Christianity.

She gave a broad smile and said, *"Yes. Praise the Lord!"*

By now Aiko had been transferred by the nurse to her hospital bed in her bedroom had slipped into sleep. I knew it was time for me to leave. I told Diane to *"Call me anytime, if I can be of help,"* and left the home.

Four days later I received a call from Diane. I learned Aiko had peacefully passed from this life. She *had achieved* her *goal* of interest; *eternal* life.

CHAPTER 8

Ain't (sic) No Dog

It was a very small house on a corner lot with a chain-link fenced yard. A sign on the gate warned "**Beware of Dog.**" From my cell phone I again called the number I had initially called to schedule the appointment I was now attempting to keep with George Swanson.

The patient was a 90 year-old male who had been admitted to a hospital four days earlier and had subsequently been diagnosed with end stage lung cancer; he had been referred to a hospice program.

The phone range three times before it was answered by the same voice I had heard earlier that day. His was a peculiar sounding voice; high pitched with a nasal twang.

"Hello, whose calling?"

"Hello again, Mr. Swanson this is the Hospice Chaplain. I'm at your gate but I see the sign about your dog," I said.

"Ain't (sic) no dog; he died. Come on in," he invited.

I unlatched the gate, entered the yard and walked to the front door which opened as I approached.

"Welcome, Chaplain. Come in if you can," he said laughing. I was surprised by what I saw. Newspapers, magazines and unopened mail sit in neat stacks around the room. On the table, sofa and floor, lined against the walls stacked almost to the ceilings. Spider webs reached from the tops of where the stacks ended connecting them to the ceiling.

I followed Mr. Swanson through a narrow pathway approximately one foot wide between the stacked piles. He led me into the bedroom which was slightly less cluttered.

"Pardon my messy house, Chaplain, I haven't been much of a house-keeper since my wife Mattie died fifteen years ago."

"Don't worry about it, we all have our idiosyncrasies," I said trying to relieve his obvious discomfort.

"Thank you for letting me see you today. How are you getting along," I asked.

"Well, I'd be a lot better off if I had given up those darn cigarettes like Mattie tried to get me to do," he replied.

"What did your doctor say about your condition, Mr. Swanson?" I asked.

"He said I had lung cancer, and that I was dying," he answered. *"Does that news frighten you?"* I asked.

"No. I can handle it. I'm a survivor; I'm 90 years-old." He was adamant in his reply.

"Do you have a religious preference? "I asked.

"No. I'm an agnostic, but my wife was a Christian," he continued.

"Do you believe in a Higher Power? I asked.

"Well, as I said, I'm an agnostic. I think, maybe, there is a God, but if there is, he doesn't want anything to do with me... but," he paused and examined his statement. *"What if I am wrong?* He answered his own question: *"If I'm wrong then I will never see my Mattie again because _ if there is a Heaven _ I know that she is there."* He stopped talking becoming silent with a distant look in his eyes as though in a trance.

Suddenly, he snapped back to reality and said, *"Excuse me for daydreaming. I was thinking about my Mattie; I miss her a lot."*

In trying to refocus his mind I said, *"Sounds like you might be thinking about trying to make a connection with a Higher Power."*

"Could be; could very well be," he replied.

For all of Mr. Swanson's idiosyncrasies, and unkempt house, I

24

was impressed with his alertness, well groomed appearance, and over all demeanor for a man who was ninety-years-of- age.

It appeared as if he suddenly wanted to be alone: He said *"I've taken too much of your time with my ramblings, Chaplain. I better let you go."* I recognized the statement as a polite way of saying goodbye.

"Before I go may I ask a couple more questions, Mr. Swanson?" I asked.

"Sure, shoot," he invited.

"Do you have a Bible?" I asked.

Yes. I have my Mattie's Bible. She used a red pen to mark it all up for me. 'Important Scriptures,' she used to say, But I haven't read it much," he continued.

"Will you do me a favor?" I asked.

"Why not?" he asked.

"Will you promise me that you will get Mattie's Bible out and read it?" I asked.

"Sure thing; I was thinking about doing it anyway," he said. *"You said you had several questions. What's your next one?"*

"First, may I come see you again? And second, may I pray with you before I leave?"

"The answer is yes to both questions," he replied.

In praying with him I asked God to grant unto him the desires of his heart, to renew his energy and strength, and give him peace.

He thanked me for the prayer. I gave him my business card and wrote my cell phone number on the back. I encouraged him to call me anytime. He thanked me again and said, *"I'll think about it."*

I never met with Mr. Swanson again. His next door neighbor and friend found him, lying face down on the floor, in the bedroom where he had spent the major part of his life since losing his wife Mattie.

The neighbor called the hospice organization that dispatched a nurse for the *"death call."*

The neighbor reported to the nurse that at the time of his death

Mr. Swanson had fallen forward and was found lying on his wife Mattie's open Bible.

A week after Mr. Swanson's death I received a small envelope simply marked *"Chaplain Curtis"* with the address scrawled in what appeared to be shaky but neat printing.

The envelope contained a thank you note with the words, *"Thank you Chaplain, I got the 'desire of my heart.' When you receive this, I will be in Heaven with Mattie."*

CHAPTER 9

Why *Not* Me?

Antonio Granatelli stood as I entered the living room. I accepted his outstretched hand in greeting.

"*You have cold hands, Chaplain,*" he said.

"Well, *you know the old saying, 'cold hands, warm heart'* I replied smiling. He laughed.

"*Good man! I like you already,*" he continued, "*have a seat so we can chat.*"

I sat down on a straight back chair next to him. He sat in a giant wall-hugger recliner.

"*Thank you for accepting my visit today,*" I began.

"*It's my pleasure, Chaplain. I'm Catholic. What is your religion?*" he asked.

"*I am non-denominational.*" I replied.

"*Nothing wrong with that,*" he said winking at me.

"*Right,*" I acknowledged, and then asked "*How are you getting along?*"

"*Pretty good,*" he answered.

"*What did your doctor say about your condition?*" I asked.

"*He said I have stomach cancer,*" he replied.

"*What does that mean to you?*" I asked.

"*It means that I'm gonna* (sic) *die. But that's O.K. I'm seventy-*

seven- years old and I've had a good life. And all my family is grown."

"You appear to be accepting the diagnosis well," I commented.

"I guess so. But you know, all my friends say 'Why you Tony? What have you done to deserve this?' But you know what? I say to them, why not me; why not you, Tony? I'm in God's hands and he knows best."

"You certainly have a good attitude toward your illness, Mr. Granatelli," I said, complimenting him. *"Call me Tony, all my friends do. Why worry? As I said I've lived a long and full life, and thank God my family is grown."*

"How many children do you have?" I asked.

"Two. A son Frank, and a daughter Nicole. They are both married and I have four Grandchildren," he continued with a facial grimace.

"Are you in pain, Tony?" I asked. *"Yeah. I think it's time for my pain medicine."* He called out to his wife Alexandria, *"Hey, honey, it's time for my medicine."*

A tall attractive. olive skinned woman responded and gave him pain medication. He introduced me to her and said, *"Honey, this is Chaplain Curtis from hospice."* She smiled her acknowledgment and quietly left the room.

"She's a great woman; very supportive," he said reaching for a glass of tomato juice sitting on a tray table next to his chair. *"Excuse me I got to take a sip of this juice to take that bitter medicine taste out of my face, "*he said laughing.

"What can I do for you today, Tony? I asked.

"Well, you can pray for me," he said.

"Have you seen a priest from your parish lately?" I asked.

"No. One came by while I was in the hospital and gave me the sacraments of the anointing (last rites) but I haven't seen the priest from my parish," he replied.

"If you would want to see a priest from your parish I could facilitate a visit for you," I offered.

"*No. My wife and daughter will take care of that,*" he responded.

I sensed that Tony was getting tired and appeared to be lethargic from the recent pain medication treatment he had received..

"*Tony, I would like to say a prayer with you, with your permission. Is that O.K.?*" I asked.

"*Sure,*" he said, "*go ahead.*" I again complimented him on his "up attitude." He smiled thanked me and said, "*Why not me; why not Tony?*" and laughed.

I said a brief prayer ending with the Our Father Prayer which we recited in unison.

I asked, "*May I have another appointment to see you again?*"

He warmly agreed by saying, "*Yes. I want you to.*"

Antonio Granatelli was admitted 911 to the hospital that evening with a cardiac arrest. He never regained consciousness. With family at his bedside, Thursday, June 9th at 3:45A.M._ one week before his seventy-eighth birthday _ Antonio "Tony" Granatelli passed from this life to the next.

CHAPTER 10

Leon's My Uncle

Early darkness was closing in as I drove up and down the residential street trying to locate and identify the numbers I was looking for. I slowly moved along the street focusing a spotlight on the house numbers. I noticed two men standing on the sidewalk visiting. One of them called out.

"What numbers you looking for?" I gave him the address and he asked, *"Is it the Brown's you're looking for?"*

"Yes. The Leon Brown residence," I told him.

He pointed to a house I had just passed and said, *"Right there. Leon is my uncle. My name is Jack."*

I glanced back at the gray stucco house whose numbers were partially hidden by a tall shrub.

"No wonder I didn't see the address," I said, in what I hoped to be a pleasant tone.

"Yeah, they need to cut down that shrub," he replied laughing.

I parked the car, walked to the door, pressed the doorbell several times and waited. There was no response.

The nephew Jack called out, *"You'll have to knock real loud, the bell don't work and his misses is hard of hearing."*

I thanked him for the information and loudly knocked on the door. At the second knock the door opened. A thin, frail woman stood before me.

"Who are you, and what do you want?" she asked.

I introduced myself as the Hospice Chaplain. I told her I was there by appointment made with husband Leon and wanted to talk with him.

She introduced herself as *"Hazel, Leon's wife. Come on in. Leon's sleeping right now."*

I entered the home and followed her into the dining room area. *"Have a seat. I'll tell him you are here,"* she said.

"Mrs. Brown, please don't wake him if he is sleeping. I can come back another time," I told her.

"Oh, he's probably awake. He's a light sleeper and our voices have probably awakened him. I'll tell him you are here," she repeated and disappeared down a hallway leading to a bed room.

She reappeared and said, *"He's awake. He wants to see you."* I followed her down the hallway to the patient's bed room

"This is the Chaplain, Leon," she said introducing me, and quickly left the room.

I observed a handsome, well groomed man who appeared to be alert and oriented.

"Good to see you, Chaplain. Thanks for coming," he said extending his hand in greeting.

"Thank you for speaking with me by phone and inviting me," I replied.

"Oh, you're welcome," he said.

"I met you nephew Jack out front," I said making small talk.

"Yeah. My sister's kid; he ain't (sic) all there," he said volunteering too much information."

"He gave me directions to your house. He seemed O.K to me," I told him.

"Yeah. Sometimes O.K., sometimes not. Anyway, you didn't come to talk about Jack. I'm hoping you came to talk about me," he replied.

"You are absolutely right, Mr. Brown. I did come to talk about you," I said.

"Good. Let's get on with it. I suppose you know what's wrong with me," he remarked in a statement question.

"Why don't you tell me," I invited.

"I have colon cancer. I have been living with it for seven years," he continued, *"The doctor now tells me that I have less than six months to live."*

"How does that make you feel," I asked.

"Well, it makes me feel like I need to get my affairs in order," he answered.

"What does that mean?" I asked.

"Well, Chaplain, I have a Durable Power of Attorney for my health care and a Living Trust for my wife, including finances, house and personal property, but I can't say I'm ready to meet my maker. That's what I want to talk about," he explained.

After a long pause he asked, *"How can you help me, Chaplain?"*

"Let's begin by asking if you have a religious preference?"

"Not to speak of," he replied.

"Have you ever gone to Sunday school or church?" I asked trying to determine his relationship to a Higher Power.

"Never went to Sunday school and never went inside a church except for weddings, and funerals," he candidly answered.

"Do you believe in a Higher Power?" I asked.

"Well, there's gotta (sic) be someone up there lookin' (sic) out for me and Hazel. We've been together for 65 years, and I'm ninety-one-years old," he said.

"So you do believe in a Higher Power?" I again asked.

"Yeah, I think so, at least want to," he said with genuine interest. He continued, *"Chaplain, you seem like a nice guy. Why don't you tell me about your religion,"* he said.

"Mr. Brown…:" he interrupted, *"Call me Leon; that's my name,"* he invited.

I began again. *"Mr. Brown… Leon, I'm more spiritual than religious, but I'll be happy to share my belief system with you."* I shared my faith from a non-denominational, main line Christendom, doctrinal perspective, as follows:

First, according to the Holy Scriptures "all mankind has sinned." Romans 3:23 Second, "the wages of sin is death" (spiritual) but "the gift of God is eternal life, through Jesus Christ the Son." Romans 6:23. Third, according to the teachings of the Scriptures, "God is not willing that any should perish (die a spiritual death), but that all should have eternal life," II Peter 3:9 In order for man to receive eternal life he must necessarily *admit* that he is a *sinner, believe* Christ died for the sins of *all* mankind (including individual sin), and *ask* for individual, personal forgiveness, through personal *invitation* to Christ. Romans 10:10 The formula for forgiveness is subjective. That is, inviting Christ into the heart and mind, and asking for personal and individual forgiveness, Ephesians 2:8-9 This is the step, by step procedure for obtaining "*eternal* Salvation," according to the teachings of the New Testament and subsequently, the majority of Christian churches known as main line Christendom. Once an individual has made the necessary preparation through this procedure they become what is known in Christian circles as "a born again," believer consistent with the Gospel of John, Chapter 3 , vvs 15-18 Someone has said, '*The Gospel of John, Chapter 3, verse 16 is the Bible in a nutshell.*'

It is quoted here: "*For God so loved the world, that he gave his only begotten Son, that whosoever believes in him should not perish, but have everlasting life.*"

To put it very simply, this is referred to as the **A, B, C's of Salvation**, (Christianity), and i.e. **Admit** sin, **Believe** in Christ, **Confess** Christ and accept Christ as *personal* Savior.

Leon Brown thanked me for the visit and information and said, "*I'll have to think about it,*" in reply to a question of, "*Does that sound like something you would like to do right now?*"

He didn't consent to a follow-up visit and I never attempted to contact him again. It is unknown whether or not he ever positively used the provided information to reach his goal of getting '*...ready to meet my (his) 'maker.*'

CHAPTER 11

I'm *Not* Gonna' (sic) Let *it Get* Me

My friend, Dr. James Goss a psychologist, and I first met when he contacted me requesting my services for one of his patients. The patient was a truck driver for a food product delivery company. It was alleged by his company that he had delivered a wrong trailer load of food items to the wrong grocery market. He was subsequently being terminated.

When confronted with the error he denied having made the delivery and claimed amnesia. Dr. James requested my service as a pastoral psychologist who also specialized in repressed memory recall through subliminal activation. The objective was to stimulate the patient's mind and break through the amnesia barrier and capture the truth.

To make a long story shorter, the patient agreed to the repressed memory recall session and the truth emerged. It was discovered that there had been a mix-up by another driver who was unaware of the wrong trailer load delivery to the wrong grocery market. Upon learning of the mistake the other driver readily took responsibility for the mix-up. The patient was *not* terminated.

Dr. James was so impressed with my therapy work that our acquaintance became a strong friendship which lasted for over twenty-five years.

At age 78 Dr. James was diagnosed with cirrhosis. A liver disease usually associated with alcohol abuse. However, this was not true in Dr. James's case. He rarely took a drink of alcohol. Sometimes he admitted to having a glass of wine with dinner.

Nevertheless, his diagnosis was advanced and terminal.

Because Dr. James was not a drinker this came as a surprise to his primary care physician and especially his family.

When I learned of his illness I contacted Dr. James and arranged a visit. At the time of my visit he had been admitted to a skilled nursing health care facility. During our visit he took my hand and said,

"I'm not gonna (sic) let this get me, Doc."

I empathized with him and attempted to support his positive attitude. At the same time, since his was a terminal diagnosis, I encouraged him to investigate a hospice program plan of care. I assured him that since I was a member of a hospice company team, I would assist him in connecting and, if he *did* meet the criteria for hospice, he should start hospice care.

On the other hand, I also explained that, if he started hospice care, and his disease didn't progress, he could revoke the service at any time.

He agreed: *"I'll give it a try,"* he said.

After having been on the hospice program for a week he was discharged from the health care facility to his home. He appeared to be gaining strength and energy.

The next time I visited Dr. James he was lying in a hospital bed, sitting in the middle of the living room of his two story condominium, where he and his wife Linda lived. He did not look good. He was pale and appeared to have lost weight.

He grasped my hand and said, *"It's so good to see you!"* He again informed me that he was *"not going to let this disease take me out."*

We chatted for a while. I could see that he was getting tired. He would occasionally nod off as he spoke. I asked if he would like a prayer, to which he agreed. I said a simple prayer ending with the our Father prayer, shook his hand and bade him good bye.

I continued to visit my friend Dr. James for the next several weeks and then received and emergency telephone call from his wife.

"Chaplain Curtis, James is asking for you," she informed me.

I responded to the call and arrived at the home. I found him to be lethargic, with decreased energy and strength. He reached for my hand.

"I wanted to see you, Doc," (he always referred to me as Doc) he said in a weak voice. "I need your prayers."

I struggled to control my emotions. Before my eyes I was seeing a long-time friend deteriorating and transitioning into death.

I held his hand and prayed with him. I anointed him with oil and offered a blessing; For spiritual support I hugged his wife and multiple family members, told them to call me if Dr. James asked for me again, and stepped into the night.

The next contact I received about my friend Dr. James was to inform me of his death. A week later, at the request of wife Linda, I conducted the funeral memorial service, held in the clubhouse, at their condominium complex.

CHAPTER 12

Until Death Do We Part

I received a call from the hospice bereavement coordinator who requested I stop by her office.

"Do you remember Rebecca Strong and Dan Noble?" she asked.

"Sure, I officiated both of their funeral memorial services," I replied. I remembered both their spouses had died on the same day. At their request, I had also conducted the memorial services the same week.

The bereavement coordinator told me, *"Their spouses Carl and Rita are both attending the bereavement support group classes. They appear to be coping well over their losses and are getting through the bereavement process appropriately."*

"Good," I replied. *"Thank you for the up-date in sharing with me. Please keep me informed of their progress."*

"I will." She promised.

She did in fact keep me informed. She kept reporting on Carl and Rita as to how they were coping in their bereavement process and how they appeared to be attracted to one another.

As they subsequently met each week for the bereavement support group she reported that it looked like they were beginning to take a serious interest in each other. How they were sitting next to each other, and how Rita reported that Carl had asked her out to lunch after a meeting.

Approximately six months into the support group class their attraction became obvious to other members. So much so that the other participants began teasing Rita and Carl saying that they *"seemed to be meant for each other."*

One year to the day, following the death of each of their spouses I received a telephone call from Carl.

"Chaplain, I would like to talk with you," he said.

"Sure, Carl. When would you like to schedule an appointment?" I asked.

"Right away," he replied.

We set an appointment day and time. I drove to his home where he greeted me with a Bear hug. He invited me in. I followed him into the living room and was not surprised to see Rita Noble present. She threw her arms around me and also warmly greeted me with a hug.

"It's so good to see you, Chaplain!" she said.

The bereavement coordinators' insight had not been misplaced. Carl and Rita wanted to discuss with me their upcoming marriage. They told me that during their time together at the bereavement support group they were attracted to each other. The attraction turned to fondness and dating which, in turn, had aroused their love and marriage interest.

One and a half years after their meeting, and getting to know one another I was privileged to perform their wedding ceremony. It appeared to be a good thing.

Out of their profound bereavement, grief and sadness over the loss of their life-long partners and soul mates, sprang forth new found hope, happiness, love, and marriage.

CHAPTER 13

That's Good; I Like That Answer

Dan Able sat on the side of his hospital bed in the bedroom of the mobile home where he and wife Carol had lived for fifteen years.

The purpose for my appointment was to offer support through a spiritual assessment.

After ten years of remission from a successful operation for liver cancer the cancer had returned.

Dan had again recently been diagnosed with liver cancer; this time inoperable.

His primary care physician had given a prognosis for the terminal illness of 3 to 6 month's duration before the illness ended in death. Subsequently, the physician had referred Dan to a hospice care program.

I met his wife Carol at the front door, introduced myself, and followed her into the bedroom. As I entered the bedroom he stood up.

He extended his hand in greeting and said, *"Let's go into the living room where it's more comfortable."*

He was using oxygen constantly with a candela nose piece attached to a long transparent tube leading to an oxygen concentrator. He held a coiled portion of the tubing in his left hand. Leaning on a cane with an unsteady walk he made his way into the living room.

Mrs. Carol Able hovered over him like a mother hen and helped him sit down into an overstuffed recliner. He gave a sigh of relief as he settled down trying to get comfortable.

"What's on your mind, Chaplain?" he asked.

"I'm here at your invitation, Mr. Able. I wanted to meet you and let me know who you are, and let you know who I am," I replied.

"That's a good answer," he said. *"It's wonderful to get to know a man of God,"* he continued.

"Do you have a religious preference?" I asked.

"Well, when I was a kid I went to Sunday school, but now, I am not very religious," he said.

"Neither am I. I am more spiritual than religious," I told him

"Yeah. I guess I could say the same thing," he said. *"What denomination was the Sunday school you attended?"* I asked.

"Oh, I don't really remember; Methodist I think," he replied.

"That's good. Do you remember what the teachings of the church were?" I asked.

"No. Not really. Something about accepting the Lord as Savior, I think," he replied.

"Is that something you ever did?" I asked him.

"No. I never did. I thought about it, but I never did," he said.

"Does it sound like something you would like to do today?" I asked.

"No. I don't believe so; I'll have to think about it," he said.

On a subsequent visit, Mr. Able insisted I call him Dan.

"Chaplain, you've got to know me pretty good. Let's do away with the formal stuff; call me Dan," he said. He then went on to say, *"I've been thinking about what you asked me on your first visit. About if I ever accepted the Lord. I'm ready to do that now. How do I go about it?"*

I explained the teachings of the Methodist church doctrine and then I was privileged to pray with him as he confessed his sin to God and invited Christ into his heart and life to become his personal Savior.

Dan Able died a week after our last visit. His wife Carol requested me to officiate his funeral memorial service. She also requested that after the funeral I stay in touch with her because she was struggling with accepting Dan's death. She had sustained a great loss; after 35 years of marriage the loss her life mate, and soul mate.

I suggested she attend a bereavement support group conducted by the hospice agency where I work. She said she would attend, and did.

For approximately a year after Dan's death I did stay in touch by telephone and learned that she was coping well in the bereavement group, where she could share her loss with others who had also lost marriage partners.

The last time I spoke with her she told me that she was moving out of state to go and live with a daughter whose husband had just been diagnosed with lung cancer. Her daughter and son in law had two pre-teen children, a boy and girl. Carol felt that she could be a strong support for them.

Carol thanked me, and the hospice bereavement support group program, for helping her recover after her loss. She believed that she could be of benefit to her daughter and son in law in sharing the experience she had gained. She looked forward to spending time with the family and especially with the grandchildren.

I encouraged her to stay in touch by phone if she needed additional support, said a prayer for her, and invoked God's blessing to go with her.

CHAPTER 14

This Too, Shall Pass

It was a warm winter day in Southern California. My assignment today was to conduct a Spiritual Assessment on a 67 year-old female who had received a recent terminal diagnosis of breast cancer.

I was met at the door by a soft-spoken silver haired man who said he was Carl, Rebecca Strong's husband. I introduced myself. He ushered me into the home and motioned me to sit down on a sofa in the living room.

"My wife is not feeling too good today," he said, and continued, *"she's been having nausea, but she insisted on seeing you."*

"My visit will be brief, Mr. Strong, it is not my intent to inconvenience her," I said.

"It's no inconvenience. She wants to see you, Chaplain," he replied.

He arose and motioned for me to go with him. I followed him down a narrow hallway and entered a darkened bed room with closed drapes. I momentarily paused to let my eyes adjust to the semi-darkness and then turned toward a hoarse voice.

"You're the Chaplain?" I heard the voice, say making a statement question.

"Yes," I replied, introduced myself and moved to the side of the hospital bed where she lay. I reached for her extended hand and was surprised at the firmness of her handshake.

"Thank you for coming, Chaplain. My name is Rebecca. Sorry about my hoarse voice. I seem to have a lot of phlegm today," she said.

I thanked her for seeing me and asked *"are you sure this is a good time for you to visit with me?"* I asked.

"Good as any, I guess," she replied. *"I wanted to see you and discuss a spiritual issue."*

"I asked for a Christian Chaplain. Are you Christian?" she asked.

"Yes. I am a Christian Chaplain, and pastor," I assured her.

"Good. The main reason I wanted to see you is because I wanted to make sure of my eternal salvation before I die," she informed me.

She explained to me that she had *"been 'saved' and had 'given her heart to the Lord, at an Oral Roberts Crusade, years ago."*

She confessed that, *"I strayed away from the Lord, and have never been very faithful."*

She explained, *"I now want to confirm my faith and re-establish my relationship with God,"*

Consistent with her Pentecostal belief system, which teaches salvation through personally inviting Christ into ones heart, I asked her if she had followed that teaching.

"Yes. That's what I did at the Oral Roberts Crusade," she said.

I explained to her that often times when a person has not connected with a particular church, and has not been a consistent and faithful attendee, that they may feel distant from God.

I suggested that sometimes a person will feel more comfortable in their relationship with God when they re-new their vows of faith. I asked her if that is something she would like to do.

"Yes, that is exactly what I want to do," she replied.

I was privileged to hold her hand and lead her in a prayer of re-dedication.

She appeared to be tiring, so I said, *"I'm pleased you let me see you today even though you were not feeling good."*

"I'm really glad you came, Chaplain, I do feel much better about my relationship with God."

I asked, *"May I see you again?"* to which she replied.

"Yes, please do. You can come and visit any time," she said.

She again took my hand, looked at me with tear-filled eyes, smiled and said, *"Don't wait to long to visit again, I don't know how much time I have left."*

I assured her I would see her again *"soon,"* walked softly out of the bedroom, and gently closed the door.

For the next three months I returned again and again during which time I established a strong rapport with both Mrs. Strong and her husband Carl.

During one of my last visits shortly before her death she requested that I officiate her funeral memorial service. I agreed stating that, *"It would be an honor and privilege for me to do so."* She smiled and said, *"You are very kind."*

Two weeks before Easter Sunday Mrs. Strong passed from this life. Her husband took her death very hard. They had been married for 53 years. I suggested he attend a bereavement support group sponsored by the hospice agency where I work. At last contact he indicated that he *was* attending the support group and, from all outward appearance, he seemed to be coping appropriately.

CHAPTER 15

Not Now; Later

At first Allen Norbert said *"Not now; later,"* to the question of *"Do you want to see a Chaplain?"* Within a week he had changed his mind, and through his hospice R.N. Case Manager requested to see a Chaplain. He was assigned to the author.

I called his home, introduced myself and, at his request, scheduled an appointment. He sounded pleased to receive my call, and was quick to set a time and date for an appointment.

I stood at the door of an attractive suburban home surrounded by neatly manicured lawns and shrubs. I rang the bell and waited for an answer.

A middle-aged woman looked through the screen and asked, *"Who are you?"* I introduced myself, after which I said, *"I have an appointment with Mr. Norbert."*

She acknowledged my introduction and said, *"I'm his sister Hazel. Come on in."* She pushed the screen door open and held it for me.

"He's *in the living room waiting for you,"* she said. I followed her through the entryway into a large sunken living room. I observed Mr. Norbert sitting on the sofa and walked toward him. He looked up from a newspaper and asked, *"You're the Chaplain?" "Yes,"* I said, and offered my hand in greeting.

"Have a seat Chaplain," he said motioning me toward a chair.

"Thanks for coming. I told the nurse I changed my mind about seeing a Chaplain. I'm glad you are here" he continued.

"Yes," I said, *"I received your message. Thank you for inviting me. How are you getting along?"*

"Pretty good, I'm taking it just one day at a time," he replied.

"What does your doctor tell you, Mr. Norbert?" I asked.

"Well, he told me I had colon cancer and that I didn't have much longer to live; three to six months," he said.

"How are you dealing with that?" I asked.

"Not very good. It was such a shock. I've never been sick a day in my life. I went through the Viet Nam War and never got a scratch and now this. I don't understand it." He stopped talking and with elbows resting on his knees put his head in his hands.

I didn't say anything for several seconds and then asked, *"Do you have a religious preference?"*

He raised his head, looked me in the eye and said, *"No, not really. I was raised in a Methodist home but religion never meant very much to me.*

"Would you like to see a Methodist minister?" I asked.

"No. You're a minister, aren't you?" I assured him I was and he said, *"You'll do. I have some questions I want to run by you, if I can"* he said.

"Sure. I will be pleased to answer them if I can," I replied.

"Chaplain, do you know what the Methodist church teaches? I never paid too much attention to it when I was a kid going to Sunday School. Then I dropped out of church when my mother died. Then I went off to Viet Nam, came home and my wife died. I never re-married and never got active in the church again," he paused in reflection.

"Sounds like you've had a lot of losses with many struggles," I said offering my empathy.

"Yeah, I guess you could say that. Now, it's my turn," he said with a quiver in his voice.

Mr. Norbert, you asked if I know what the Methodist church

46

teaches. Yes. The Methodist church is mainline Christendom. This means that they teach basic mainline Christian doctrine.

Would you want me to explain that doctrine," I asked.

"Yes. I'd like that," he replied.

MY EXPLANATION:

"The Methodist church doctrine comes from the New Testament and teaches that man is a sinner by choice, and that God sent his Son Jesus to planet earth to die for the sins of mankind.

This was so that man did not have to die a physical death for his own personal sin. In other words, Christ became a one-time sacrifice for the redemption of mankind. The Methodist church affirms that since man is a sinner by choice God has provided a sin atonement through his Son Jesus Christ at the Cross of Calvary. Further, their doctrine teaches that man _ in order to receive forgiveness _ must (it is imperative) go to God through the Son Jesus Christ. That is to say, man is saved by God's grace, through man's faith: you must believe it, to receive it. And, that salvation comes through a spiritual awakening by man who, through admission of personal sin ,a belief that God will forgive him, and confession (invitation) to Christ to become his personal savior. This is referred to by Christians as 'God's Plan of Salvation.'

It is also known by Christians as the A, B, C's of Salvation, or Christianity.

Therefore, according to the doctrinal teachings of the mainline Christian faith there are three steps involved in order to obtain God's forgiveness and Salvation. They are:

ADMIT: *Admit that you are a sinner according to the Bible, Romans 3:23, "All have sinned and come short of the glory of God."*

BELIEVE: *Believe that Christ did, in fact, die for the sins of mankind, including individual personal sin, and then...*

CONFESS: *Christ as Messiah and Savior by inviting him _ with the mouth to come into the heart and mind and forgive personal sin, thus,* *saving the individual soul. This, according to the New Testament, Ephesians, Chapter 2, vvs 8-9. KJV "For by grace are you saved through faith; and that not of yourselves: it is the gift of God. 9 Not of works, lest any man should boast." And, Romans, Chapter 10, vvs 9-10. KJV "That if thou shalt confess with your mouth the Lord Jesus, and shalt believe in thine heart that God hath raised him from the dead, thou shalt be saved. 10 For with the heart man believeth unto righteousness; and with the mouth confession is made unto salvation.*

I paused for effect after my explanation and, for his processing what had been explained, then asked, *"Does any of this sound familiar to you?"*

He smiled and replied, *"Yes. Some of what you said is starting to come back. It's beginning to make sense."*

I followed up by asking, *"Mr. Norbert, does this sound like something you have ever done? Have you made a personal commitment to Christ according to the teaching of your own religious denomination?"*

"No. No, I can't say that I ever have," he answered.

"Does this sound like something that you would like to do?" I asked.

"Yes." He replied, *I'd like to do that." How do I go about it?"*

I was pleased to be able to pray with Mr. Norbert a simple prayer, asking him to repeat the prayer _ if the words being prayed expressed the desire of his heart _ repenting of his sin and asking God's forgiveness.

I kept my eyes open as we prayed; tears of emotion slid down his cheeks as he voiced the prayer requesting forgiveness and inviting Christ into his heart as personal Savior.

At the conclusion of the prayer he gripped my hand in a firm handshake and said two words. *"Thank you."*

Mr. Norbert followed me to the door and asked, *"When can I see you again?"*

I was pleased to tell him, that with his permission, *"I can visit on a weekly basis."*

"Good," he said. *Next time I want to talk about my funeral memorial service,"* and started to tear up again.

"Thank you for seeing me today Mr....." he stopped me and said, *"Call me Allen, Chaplain."*

I continued, *"Thank you for seeing me today, Allen, I will be calling to set an appointment for next week."*

"No need to call, just come on over," he invited

"Thank you, Allen, I will see you next week," I replied.

He stood at the door and waved to me as I drove out of sight.

Over the next several months I returned weekly to visit with him. We were able to plan his funeral memorial service _ which he asked me to officiate _ to which I consented. He asked me to baptize him and we shared holy communion several times.

At one of our last visits he said, *"I consider you to be my pastor."*

I thanked him and told him *"I thought of him as a good man and a friend."*

Early on a Friday morning I received a call that Allen Norbert was *"actively dying, and that his sister Hazel was asking for me."*

I drove to the home and was met by his sister Hazel. She led me to the bedside of Allen. His eyes were closed and he appeared to be resting comfortably. He aroused and opened his eyes when I softly called his name. He seemed to recognize me and said in a whisper voice, *"Thank you. I'll see you again in Heaven."* He then appeared to lapse into a semi-comatose state. I reached for his hand. I detected a faint response when I said, *"Allen, if you can hear me squeeze my hand."*

I told Hazel that *"hearing was the last faculty we lose the ability to use, and that I was going to talk to Allen as if he was hearing every word I was saying, and very well may be."*

I read some Scripture from the Psalms ending with the 23rd Psalm and then invited Hazel to join hands with me as we prayed the Our Father prayer. I then blessed Allen and anointed him with oil.

With his sister Hazel sitting at his bedside Allen Norbert passed from this life with a peaceful death at 1:44 P.M.

According to the teachings of the Scriptures, which says and I quote, "*...to be absent from the body...*" (is) "*to be present with the Lord,*" KJV 2 Corinthians 5:8; his spirit went to be with God, to rest and abide in that place not made with hands, eternal in the heavens.

CHAPTER 16

I'm *Gonna'* (sic) Beat This Thing

Thin would be an understatement for the 97 year-old cancer patient I was visiting. She extended her hand in greeting and said, *"Thank you for coming to see me, Chaplain."*

She introduced herself as Sally Young and continued, *"I guess you already know I have lung cancer from smoking cigarettes. The doctor said I'm going to die in 3 to 6 months, but I'm gonna beat it. I've been praying to God for a miracle to heal me."*

In clinical language the patient was holding onto what is called denial, with unrealistic expectations, unless, of course, she did receive her *"miracle."* In this particular case it could be termed "informed denial" since the patient knew that her diagnosis was terminal. She knew exactly what her diagnosis was, yet she chose to deny it, and continued to pray for a healing miracle.

For Mrs. Young, due to the advanced stage of her lung cancer, it appeared to be unrealistic to expect a miracle.

Conversely, it is important for the reader to know, miracles do sometimes happen when a patient goes into remission after receiving chemotherapy and radiation. However, by her own admission, Mrs. Young had not improved with either.

Subsequently, her medical doctor had diagnosed her with a terminal illness, with a 3 to 6 month life expectancy, and referred her to a hospice program for palliative care. She was now experiencing post-diagnostic shock, and was in denial refusing to mentally accept her life threatening disease, in spite of her weakening physical condition, caused by the cancer which had already ravaged her body and health.

Wanting to set her mind at ease by moving in another direction, and trying to obtain a profile on her spiritual perspective, I asked, *"What is your religious preference?"*

"I'm Protestant, Non-denominational," she replied.

"Are you connected to a church right now?" I continued.

"No," she said, *"I used to go on a regular basis, but I haven't gone steady since moving to California."*

"How long have you lived in California," I asked.

"Thirty-one years," she replied, *"But I want to get closer to God again."*

"What can I do for you today, Mrs. Young," I asked.

"Well, you can pray for me, Chaplin. Pray that God will heal me. With both of us praying, along with my family and friends, I am sure he will hear us and surely heal me." Mrs. Young, I will pray that God will grant unto you the desire of your heart. However, I hesitate to pray for your physical healing, because healing comes in more than just the physical. God can give us healing of the emotions _ emotional healing _ spiritual healing, and healing causing peace of mind. Do you want me to pray God will give you the desire of your heart?"

"Yes, please do," she consented.

I was pleased to also read some Scriptures of comfort and assurance for Mrs. Young and say some prayers. I asked her to join me in reciting the Our Father prayer.

"Thank you for your visit, Chaplain. Will you come and see me again?" she asked.

"It would be my pleasure," I said and told her I would always call ahead to schedule another appointment.

Two weeks later on my second visit Mrs. Young had obviously declined. She appeared to have lost weight and was struggling with breathing.

"Chaplain," she said, *"I'm so weak; I' getting weaker every day. I don't think God is listening to our prayers."*

"Mrs. Young, God is always listening to our prayers. There are three answers to prayer:

Yes, No, and Wait," I told her, in what I hoped was a pleasant and conciliatory voice.

"Call me Sally, Chaplain, everybody else does," she invited, and continued, *"I guess he's saying 'no' ' cause I sure can't wait much longer if he's gonna'* (sic) *heal me,"* she replied.

"Mrs. Young... Sally, God never calls one of his kids home to Heaven until he is ready for them," I assured her.

"I wish he would make up his mind," she replied.

"He has Sally; when he is ready," I told her.

"If he isn't going to heal me, then I wish he would call me home to Heaven," she said almost pleadingly.

I could tell from her conversation that she was slowly moving away from denial and toward accepting her life-threatening illness. I read Scripture to her, said some prayers, offered a blessing and an anointing with oil. I assured her I would soon come again, and bade her "bye for now."

Approximately one week later she called my office and left a message that she wanted to see me. I called her home and spoke with a granddaughter who informed me that, *"Grandma is in the hospital.."* I asked *"Why?"* she had gone to the hospital. All the granddaughter knew was that *'Grandma had been having trouble breathing.'* I called the hospital and learned that she had been 'admitted through the Emergency Room for respiratory distress,' and was 'in ICU.'

I made a brief visit with her at the hospital. She was using 02 (oxygen) continuously at the time of my visit and appeared to be breathing comfortably. She told me she was being discharged back to her home the next day.

I prayed a short prayer with her, and told her I would see her for a longer visit at her home. She smiled, squeezed my hand and said, *"O.K."*

Two days later I again paid her a visit. She appeared to have increased strength, and energy. She said, *"I feel so much better today. Maybe God is going to give me a healing miracle."*

Sally was more talkative than I had ever observed her to be. She said, *"Oh, I'm so glad you came to see me today. I hope I didn't inconvenience you."*

"No, not at all, Sally _ you said I could call you by your first name..." she interrupted me. *"Yes. I want you to call me Sally,"* she said confirming her original request.

"I'm glad you are feeling better today. You seem to have increased energy and strength," I said to her.

"Yes, but I don't know for how long," she replied.

"Enjoy it while you can, one day at a time," I encouraged her. We spent another forty- five minutes together. I read Scripture, offered her holy communion and prayed with her. She thanked me profusely and asked, *"When will I see you again?"*

"I'll be back in a few days to check on you, Sally. In the meantime, if you need to see me before I call you, to schedule another appointment, please call; O.K,?" I asked her.

"Sure, Chaplain. Thanks again for coming to see me again," she continued, *"see ya (sic)' soon; good bye for now."*

It appeared at this visit Sally was experiencing what we term in hospice language as a "burst of energy." Some patients experience multiple burst of energy; one day alert and aware, with increased energy and strength; the next lethargic and barely responsive.

Sally was a classic example of one of those patients. For over six months I observed her to be up and down the energy scale.

On my last visit Sally was having a good day and appeared to be filled with energy.

However, as we visited I could discern her energy ebbing and she was becoming lethargic. She would nod off in the middle of a sentence. Finally she aroused and said, *"You know, Chaplain, this is no life. I just want to die. I'm tired of being sick.*

I empathized with her and said a prayer. She was sleeping when

I left her home. Lori, Sally's granddaughter and primary caregiver, let me out, and asked,

"How long do you think grandma has to live?"

I told her, *"in my opinion, not very long. I believe she is actively dying."* I suggested she *"call other family members so they could be present and supportive when, and if, Sally did* pass." She said she would.

That night, Sally's "wish" was granted; at 10:40 P.M. God called her *home*.

CHAPTER 17

I Want to *Catch Up* My Dues

Ms. Clarice Austin was a 92 year-old breast cancer patient who had been admitted to the hospice program where I serve as Chaplain. During the time she was being evaluated for hospice appropriateness in being brought on service she had indicated that she did want to see a Chaplain.

Subsequently, her case was assigned to me, and I was notified of her request. When I initially met her she was a resident in a health care facility. I met her at bedside and introduced myself, whereupon, she extended her hand in greeting and said, *"Oh, thank you for coming to see me, Chaplain."*

I told her it was "my pleasure," and asked, *"How can I be of help to you?"*

"Well, Chaplain," she said, *"I have not been a very good Christian. I have let other things get in the way of my going to church. May God forgive me."* She ended the conversation short of breath and adjusted the 02 (oxygen) nose piece, called a candela, in an attempt to get more air and ease her breathing.

I hastened to tell her to *"take your time, and try not to talk too much. Rather, just let me do the talking, and you answer with a nod or head shake."* She nodded her head but said, *"I need to talk. I'll be all right, just let me catch my breath."*

After resting for a few minutes she began again. *"Chaplain, my first Cousin and a Niece are my only living relative. I've outlived all the others. My Cousin wants me to go to an assisted living facility, because, as sick as I am, I'm not sick enough to be in a nursing home. So my Cousin is making plans to place me in a board and care home. That's O.K. with me because, I don't want to be a burden to my Cousin. Of course, I will miss my independence, limited though it is,"* she stopped talking and waited for my response.

I was very impressed with the alertness, acuity and clarity of thinking by the 92 year old patient who had recently been diagnosed with a terminal illness of uterine cancer.

I did the only thing I knew how to do, under the circumstances, I asked, *"How can I help?"* *"Well, since I don't have a pastor, the first thing I need to know is that you will still be able to see me wherever I end up,"* she said.

"Please know that you will be my patient, and I will see you wherever you go," I assured her.

"Good. That's good to know. Then I will consider you as my pastor." she said, *"In the meantime, you can pray for me."*

"I'll be pleased to do that, Ms. Austin, but would you like for me to facilitate a minister from a Christian church to come and pray with you?" I asked.

"No," she replied, *"you are the only minister I need. I only want to see you."*

I thanked her for her confidence, read some Scripture from the Psalms to her, prayed with her, and anointed her with oil.

"Oh, I feel so much better, Chaplain," she said. *"You are so kind. Thank you. Thank you for seeing me today."*

"Thank you, for seeing me. I will be in touch, and I will know where you will be transferred to," I assured her, and bade her good bye.

The next time I saw Clarice Austin she was a resident in a board and care facility. Her condition had changed remarkably. Whereas, just two weeks before she had been ambulatory, alert without confusion, with her self-care well managed, today, she was bed bound, and spoke in a small, weak voice little more than a whisper. Nevertheless, she insisted on talking and informing me of her immediate concerns. She held my hand and spoke haltingly.

"Chaplain, I was a member of the Eastern Star for 35 years and then I let my dues lapse. I would like to catch up my dues before I die. Also, I would like for an Eastern Star funeral ritual at my funeral memorial service, along with you," she paused to catch her breath and then continued, *"You will officiate at my funeral, won't you?"*

I assured her I would *"consider it an honor to officiate her memorial service."*

"Can you contact my niece Louise, who is also in the Eastern Star, and check out for me whether they can conduct the funeral ritual at my service?" She asked.

"I would be pleased to do that, Mrs. Austin..." she held up her hand and said, *"Call me Clare for Clarisse, please."*

I began again. *"I would be pleased to do that Clare. I will get some details about the Eastern Star and call your niece to see if we can get it arranged."*

"One more thing, Chaplain," She continued, *"see this ring?"* she held up her hand. My eyes were drawn to a sterling silver Eastern Star ring with a diamond set in the center. *"Yes. That is a beautiful ring,"* I told her.

"Thank you. I want to give this ring to one of the Eastern Star candidates who can't afford one. Please include that in the information you give to my niece," She concluded her requests.

I assured her I would honor her requests. I noticed that she was getting very tired. I began bringing my visit to a close..

"Mrs. Austin," I said, and then remembered she wanted me to call her 'Clare,' *Clare, I sense that you are getting tired. Would you want me to say some prayers for you before I go?"*

"Oh, please do, Chaplain," she invited.

I held her hand and said some prayers ending with the Our Father prayer. I then offered her a blessing, and anointed her with oil.

Clare said, *"Thank you very much, Chaplain, you have given me peace of mind."*

"You are very welcome, Clare, It has been my pleasure," I told her.

She weakly squeezed my hand, closed her eyes and slid into sleep. I gently withdrew my hand from hers and quietly left the room.

The next day I learned from the primary caregiver that, with dignity and a peaceful mind, Clarice Austin passed from this life at 4:24 P.M.

CHAPTER 18

I've Been *Hurting* for a *Long* Time

His name was John Slimmer, his age 55 years; the terminal illness liver cancer. I arrived at the home at his request for a spiritual assessment evaluation. I introduced myself as the Hospice Chaplain. He shook my hand with a firm grip. From all outward appearances he looked to be very healthy. From his looks no one would have suspected that John was dying from a terminal illness. A disease he had contracted, by his own admission, *"from wild living, alcohol, drugs and party-going."* His official diagnosis was cirrhosis of the liver, alcohol related.

During our conversation he told me that he had *"abused alcohol and drugs. As a result of his sharing needles he had also contracted hepatitis B,"* a disease he had lived with for twenty-five years.

The fear of the disease being contagious had alienated him from family and friends. And now because of heavy alcohol abuse he was paying a greater price.

He told me he was getting along *"pretty good, except for having blackouts."* He demonstrated what he meant. He said, *"I seem to want to blackout every time I bend over to pick up my bag of drugs (medications) and take out what I need; the one's I'm supposed to take, I get dizzy and blackout. For the last couple of days I have found myself waking up with my head touching the bed and my body bent over the bed."* He again demonstrated.

He went on to say, *"I think this is from the long-term hepatitis B. from which, I've been hurting for a long time. I don't want to hurt anymore,"* he concluded.

The hospice nurse arrived during my visit and we cut our conversation short. I said a short prayer, at his request, and assured him I would visit with him again soon. I left my business card and told him *"if you need to see me, or talk, feel free to call and another appointment will be made."*

He thanked me for my time and said, *"Please do come back and visit with me any time, Chaplain. I enjoy your company and feel better each time you visit."*

I shook his hand, and suggested that he discuss his *"black outs"* with the nurse, and told him *"good bye for now,"* and let myself out of the home.

Over the next several months John and I spent time together talking, reading Scripture and praying. He told me time and again that, *"I really enjoy your (my) company, and your coming to visit."*

During the course of our discussions I learned that he had been married and divorced. That he had siblings, and some faithful friends with whom he was still in contact. He repeatedly told me that *"I don't want to be a burden to anybody,"* and, *"I want to stay busy to take my mind off myself."*

The more we talked at on-going appointments the more John took me into his confidence. He began to really open up with life review. He told me about his thirteen year marriage and his step-fatherhood. He said, *"I married a woman with an 8 month old baby,"* and how *"I grew very fond of the baby and thought of her as my own flesh and blood."* He went on to tell me that. *"My wife Millie spoiled Julie rotten and let her do just about anything she wanted to do. She never wanted me to discipline or correct Julie. She always said that I 'was not her father and that it was not right for me to try and correct her.'"*

He explained that, *"this was the ultimate cause for a mutually agreed upon divorce."* He continued, *"I think that because of my influence in her young life, she turned out pretty good. Today she has her life turned around and is a good kid."* He smiled as he let his thoughts turn back to step-daughter Julie.

John did stay busy. On numerous occasions he was not at home when I called to schedule an appointment. When I did catch him at home he would say. *"I'm going to my sister's,"* or *"I'm with a friend,"* etc.

When I did catch him at home he would often say, *"I wanna'* (sic) *get closer to the Lord."*

During those visits we would always pray together and more than once he wanted to renew his vows of faith, and rededicate his life to Christ as Savior.

On one of our last visit, John talked about his parents. His father had been an alcoholic and had died when he was only 8 years old. His mother and grandmother had raised him and his siblings. He talked about how his mother had made a list of things she had owned and had assigned a name to every item of her property. He told me she had said, *"I'm doing this so that there would not be any arguments after I'm gone."* A tear rolled down his cheek as he spoke.

He went on to say, *"I'm doing the same thing with my personal belongings,"* and with his arm he made a sweeping gesture of the room. With a sigh he said, *"My life has been reduced to everything that's in this bed room,"* which he was renting from a landlord. I glanced around the room. It contained a bed, nightstand, TV with stand, a dresser, table lamp, and small table with two chairs.

John said, *"This represents 55 years of living,"* and then said, *enough of this, Chaplain. Why don't you pray with me?"*

I was pleased to pray with, and for, John. I asked God *"To grant unto him the desire of his heart not to be a burden to anyone, or, to hurt anymore, and to give him peace,"* I closed with the Our Father prayer which John recited with me.

"Thank you, Chaplain, I know God is listening," John said. I shook his hand, told him to call me if he needed to see me, or talk, and told him *"Good-bye for now."*

I believe God *was* listening. That evening, John closed his eyes in sleep never to awaken.

CHAPTER 19

*Now, I'm *Ready* to Go...*

Mr. Arnold Thomas was a fail man and appeared to be skin and bones. In medical terms, a condition called "cachectic."

The day I met him he had just been discharged from the hospital where he had been admitted for a heart condition. He had sustained a severe CVA (a medical term for a major stroke). According to the family, this had been his third attack and his doctor had diagnosed him with a myocardial infarction, a terminal disease, and had referred him to the hospice program where I serve as Chaplain..

At the time of my visit Mr. Thomas was using 02 (oxygen) continuously and was struggling to talk above a whisper. Not wanting him to use too much energy I phrased my communication with him so he could answer for the most part with a yes or no answer. I had been told that his religious preference was Baptist, so after the initial introduction and small talk I came directly to the point and segewayed to the topic of my visit; spiritual support.

"I understand you are Baptist," I said. He nodded. I asked him, *"Are you connected to a local church?"*

He answered, *"No."*

I then asked, *"Would you like for me to facilitate a Baptist clergy person to your home for prayers and on-going spiritual support?"* He emphatically said, *"No!"*

I then asked, *"Do you remember what the Baptist church teaches about your relationship to the lord?"*

Again his answer was, *"No. I'm not very religious."*

I asked, *"Would you like for me to explain the doctrinal teachings of the Baptist church?"*

He was silent for a few minutes and then said, *"Yes. I would like that."*

I explained the doctrinal teachings of the Baptist church. That is, the acknowledgment of personal sin, asking God for forgiveness, and inviting Christ into the heart as personal Savior, and the assurance of forgiveness, followed by eternal life after life; eternal life.

With rapt attention and interest, Mr. Thomas appeared to hang on my every word. After my explanation I asked, *"Have you ever made a commitment to Christ consistent with the teaching of your own church."*

He replied, *"No, I can't say that I have."*

I then asked, *"Does this sound like something you would like to do? Invite Christ into your heart, to forgive your sin, and save your soul?"*

He thought about the question for several minutes and then said, *"Yes, I would like to do that."*

With bowed head, I was privileged to lead him in a prayer reflecting the desire of his mind and heart."

Speaking with emotion and tear-filled eyes he said, *"Now, I'm ready to go."* The hidden meaning, he was prepared to die.

Mr. Thomas and I enjoyed several more visits following that initial visit. I was privileged when he asked, *"Will you be my pastor?"* I told him, *"I would be pleased to be your pastor."*

As his disease progressed, and he became bed bound, I felt even more privileged when, two days before his death he asked, *"Will you officiate my funeral service when I die?"*

I assured him, *"I would consider it an honor."*

Three months to the day, after entering the hospice program, surrounded by family holding his hand, Mr. Thomas died a peaceful death.

CHAPTER 20

Short time; Sweet Spirit

On a Monday morning, from my voice mail, I learned of Mrs. Ruth Hale's start of care as a hospice patient. The R.N., who had brought her on service, stated that the patient was from England and that her religious preference was Episcopal; she wanted to see a Chaplain.

I called her home to set an appointment. She answered the phone with a heavy British accent.

"Hello, this is Ruth Hale, who's ringing me up?" she asked.

I answered, *"This is Curtis, the hospice Chaplain. I understand you requested to see a Chaplain."*

"Yes, Chaplain" she replied, *"When do you want to see me?"* she asked.

"At your convenience, Mrs. Hale; when would be a convenient day and time?" I asked.

"What about this afternoon, Chaplain?" she invited.

"Sure, what time?" I asked.

"How does 3:30 sound to you, Chaplain?" she asked.

"That's fine. I'll be pleased to see you at 3:30 Mrs. Hale," I replied.

"Call me Ruth, Chaplain," she said, *"let's not be too formal."*

"O.K., then, I'll see you this afternoon," I told her.

I arrived at her home and was surprised to see that her appearance almost perfectly matched the image I had formed of her as we spoke on the phone. She was tall and thin with red hair, but her voice seemed to be lower than it had sounded on the telephone.

According to the medical history she had been diagnosed with ovarian cancer and had lost twenty-five pounds in the past 6 months. The diagnosis had been given eleven months earlier. Her affect was pleasant and her soft brown eyes appeared kind. She extended her hand in greeting. Her grip was warm, sweaty, and limp.

"I'm Episcopal, Chaplain," she offered. She invited me to sit down at the dining room table where she joined me.

"Good," I replied, *"Are you connected to a local parish?"* I asked.

"Yes. I belong to St. Andrews Episcopal," She answered. St. Andrew parish was very close to her residence.

"Is your pastor visiting?" I asked.

"He's on vacation right now. But he would visit if I asked him," she continued.

"When does he return from vacation; do you know?" I asked.

"Yes. Two more weeks," she answered.

"Is there an assistant pastor?" I asked.

"No. It's a small parish," she replied.

"Would you like for me to call the church secretary and give her a message with her that you want to see the pastor when he gets back from vacation?" I asked.

"Yes. I would like that," she replied.

During our visit her husband came into the dining room. She introduced me.

"Peter, this is Chaplain Curtis." He shook my hand and said, *"It's good to meet you. It's nice of you to come visit,"* and quickly left the room.

I sensed that Ruth was getting tired so I asked, *"Would you like for me to say some prayers with you?"*

She replied, *"Please do."* After praying with her she made a bold statement.

She calmly said, *"I know I'm dying, Chaplain. It's just a matter of time as to when."*

The next time I visited with Ruth Hale she had changed remarkably. She appeared to have lost weight; her complexion was pale and she was noticeably weaker, with decreased energy. It was difficult to recognize her as the same person.

She told me that her pastor had returned from vacation and he had visited her. She thanked me for facilitating the visit. At the time, I didn't know, that this would be my last visit with her.

The following week I learned that she had sustained a minor stroke, a CVA; a medical abbreviation for Cardio Vascular Accident, and had been taken by paramedics to a local hospital.

In subsequent weeks, I learned that she had been DC'd (discharged) from the hospital and had relocated to her sister's home in South Dakota. Four days after her relocation, I learned from her sister, with a peaceful death she had passed away in her sleep.

A week later I received a call from her sister Mildred. *"Chaplain Curtis, I want to thank you for being a friend and a pastor to my sister Ruth. In the short time we had together, after she came to live with me, she spoke highly of you, and shortly before her death she said, 'Tell the hospice Chaplain Curtis, I'm glad he visited me.'"*

CHAPTER 21

Love, Prescription for Forgiveness

The bright August sun climbed steadily into a smog filled sky. An alternating clock- thermometer mounted on a wall in front of the doctor's medical suite showed the temperature to be 88%. It was going to be another hot, muggy day in sunny Southern California. The clock flashed the time at just past 7 A.M.

I parked, locked my car, and entered the community hospital where I served as a Chaplain. I was scheduled to see a patient who had just been started on hospice care and was requesting to see a Chaplain. I walked through the doctor's lounge grabbing a cup of black coffee and a doughnut on the way to my office.

I walked toward room 139 where Mr. Nugent, the patient I was scheduled to see, had been taken. Arriving at the room I noted an isolation alert sign posted outside the door. It read, *"Cap, gown, gloves and mask required."* After gloving, masking, and gowning up, I looked inside the room. The small- framed man lying on the bed, identified on the name plate outside the room as Roger Nugent, appeared to be sleeping. I decided not to disturb him.

At the nurse's station I conferred with the charge nurse and learned the man in room 139 had been diagnosed with Acquired Immune Deficiency AIDS; it was also learned he had full blown AIDS.

I glanced at the wall clock. By this time I noted that it was 11 a.m.

I knew he would be awakened for lunch. I quickly made a decision to eat early and then visit him afterwards.

The telephone was ringing when I walked back into my office. The voice of the Station One charge nurse spilled into my ear.

"Chaplain, Mr. Nugent's sister is here. She wants to talk with you. Her name is Carol Thompson. She's in the waiting room; will you see her there or in your office?" she asked.

"Tell her I will see here in the waiting room," I told her.

The waiting room was dark except for the dim glow coming from a lamp on a corner table. When I entered a dark haired, pale-faced woman eagerly looked up.

"I'm Carol. Are you the..." she hesitated, as tears brimmed in her eyes. I sat on the couch next to her and placed my hand on her shoulder, waiting. She reached into her purse, pulled out a worn, wet tissue and brushed away the tears.

"Would you see my brother?" She asked her voice breaking. She gained momentary control and continued, *"You see, Chaplain, I'm the only one he has. The rest of the family has abandoned him."*

Sensing the need for privacy I invited her to the chaplain's office. She appeared calmer after I offered her a glass of water, and placed a box of tissue in front of her. Trying hard to hold back tears she began to talk hesitantly and to share the family history.

She said, *"Mr. Nugent _ Roger had 'come out of the closet' seven years ago and had moved in with a significant other. The conservative family members went ballistic and traumatically moved through symptoms of anger, disbelief, shock, and finally abandonment,"*

She paused to gain composure and continued. *"Within the past two years Roger has been rejected by his lover of nine years, and is now actively dying with AIDS."*

Carol shared with me, that she had not found the courage to face her mother and other family members with the truth of his hospitalization and imminent death. Tears freely flowed as the story unfurled. Carol shared her concerns as to her Brother Roger's relationship with God, and the security of his soul as the time of his death approached. She finished talking and asked, *"Can we go see him now?"* I nodded assent and stood as she exited the office and walked down the hall toward room 139.

Roger looked up when we walked into the room. Wearing masks, gowns and gloves (more for his protection than our own) Roger had difficulty recognizing his sister Carol, until she spoke. She introduced me, *"Roger, this is Chaplain Curtis. I've asked him to see you."*

His eyes lighted up. I extended a hand in greeting and then placed it on his shoulder. His sister crept from the room. We were alone.

He stared directly into my face and asked, *"Chaplain, will you call...,"* he stopped talking, tears filling his eyes. I reached for his hand and held it waiting for him to continue.

He soon began again. *"Will you call my mother? Tell her I'm in the hospital. Tell her I am dying, and that I want to see her."* His breathing quickened; he gripped my hand. His face was tense expressing a sense of urgency. *"Will you call her right away, please? My sister says she can't talk to my mother about me. She will listen to you, Chaplain. Will you call her as soon as possible?"*

"Yes, I will call her for you, but before I make the call, may I pray with you?" I asked.

"Yes. Pray for me, and my mother," he invited.

"What would you have me pray for, Roger?" I asked waiting to give him control over the prayer.

I flipped open a small notebook and wrote as he spoke:

A Prayer from Roger, For My Mother, Mary. I pray that my mother can forgive me, as I have forgiven her. I pray that she can know I love her, as I know she loves me. Your son, Roger

Finishing his prayer he lay back on the bed exhausted. *"I'll call her at once,"* I said reassuringly, and squeezed his hand. I spoke words of encouragement, *"Now, more than anything else, you need to get some rest."*

His lonely and pleading gaze met mine. I was touched by his young, blue-green eyes of 29 years, trapped in a disease ridden and ravaged face that appeared to be twice his tender age.

I walked back to my office and sat at my desk collecting my thoughts and reflecting on the conversation with Roger about his mother. I struggled with my own emotion for several minutes before picking up the phone.

I called medical records, got his mother's number, and dialed. A questioning voice answered. *"Yes. Who's calling?"*

I tried to sound calm and spoke in a soft voice. *"Mrs. Nugent..."* I began, and was interrupted.

"My name is not Nugent. It's Carlson; I've re-married," she said.

I started over. *"Mrs. Carlson, my name is Chaplain Curtis Smith at the local community hospital. I am calling about your son, Roger. He asked me to call you. He was admitted to the hospital last night. His condition has worsened. He's asking for you."*

Her demanding voice screamed into the phone, *"He's not dead, is he?"* It was more a painful plea for reassurance than a question.

"No, Mrs. Carlson, his condition appears to be stable, for now." There was silence: I thought she had hung up until I heard her voice again.

"Tell him to hang on, don't let him die, Chaplain," she begged.

I tried to give her comfort. *"He's getting the best available medical care..."* She again interrupted.

"Did my daughter talk to you, Chaplain?" She didn't pause to let me answer. *"Did Carol tell you that Roger and I don't get along? That we haven't spoken in over nine years? We had a big disagreement over his life-style. All these years I wanted to go to him so he could ask for my forgiveness. The last thing I remember saying to him was, "Get out of my house! I never want to see you again!"*

Her voice broke. I listened to her agonizing sobs. Tears clouded and stung my own burning eyes. A mother and son so alienated and lost to each other. I said a silent prayer for the mother who appeared to be so hard. *"Please God; help her find forgiveness in her heart to heal this broken relationship."*

"Tell him I'm coming; I'm on the way," she said. The click of the broken connection was followed by a dial tone.

I joined Carol in the hospital cafeteria. *"Roger asked me to call your mother. She's on the way to the hospital,"* I told her.

"Oh, my God! I hope she doesn't make a scene!" she replied, struggling to control her tears.. I breathed a silent prayer, *"Dear Heavenly Father, please let the mother and son reconcile their differences with forgiveness."*

Carol shoved away the salad she had been picking at and stood up. Together we walked down the hallway to room 139. Opening the door we saw the room was empty. At the same time the toilet flushed in the bathroom. Roger was in there. We walked back into the waiting hallway, entered the waiting room and sat down, hoping Roger and Carol's mother would soon arrive.

Within fifteen minutes the mother stood in front of us. She and Carol embraced and stood silently holding one another for several minutes. After introductions we all walked back to room 139. Opening the door we again observed that the room was empty. I stepped to the bathroom and opened the door. Roger lay face down, on the floor, motionless. I looked through the door back into the room and saw Roger's mother Mary's ashen face. I quickly escorted her and Carol from the room seating them in the waiting room. With lightning speed I notified the charge nurse, who in turn, hastily activated a code by calling the switchboard. Within seconds a **"Code Blue! Code Blue, Room 139 STAT!"** was sounding throughout the hospital over the sound system.

I returned to Carol and Mary who were anxiously pacing the floor just outside room 139. We watched while doctors, nurses, and technicians hurried down the hall and hastened into the room carrying and pushing emergency equipment.

I again breathed a silent prayer: *"God, please make some sort of sense out of this for Mary. Help her to find forgiveness for her son, Roger.*

While the hospital team worked with Roger I suggested we go to the hospital chapel to pray.

Twenty minutes later a doctor who had been inside room 139

only minutes before stood in front of us. His grim look made a bold statement before he started talking. In a soft voice the doctor explained what had happened.

"An internal aneurism burst, throwing his already weakened system into shock causing his heart to stop beating in a full cardiac arrest. Over and over we tried to resuscitate him. But nothing; No response; we did all we could to save him, but we lost him." The doctor said," *I'm sorry,"* then moved out of the chapel leaving the family in stunned silence.

"God, how could this happen? Why" I, too, was stunned. I looked out the window. Heat waves danced off the black-top parking lot. The hot weather had pushed the thermometer past the 98 degree mark. In spite of the heat, a cold chill raced up my back. I glanced at Mary and Carol. A grief-stricken, sad and forlorn look reflected in their faces; their eyes held a wounded look. They were processing the news. The son and brother was gone; he had passed from life to death. I heard myself saying, *"I'm very sorry."* The words seemed so pitifully inadequate.

Finally, Mary spoke, *"Chaplain, I loved my son, I only hated his life-style,"*

I again turned to God in silent prayer. *"Please, God, give Mary and Carol the physical strength, the mental alertness, and spiritual maturity they need in this time of trauma and loss."*

Almost simultaneously both mother and daughter turned to me and asked, *"When can we see him?"*

I walked down the corridor with them knowing that this was a very normal request for family members to request to spend time with the body of the loved one after they had died. It was a form of accepting reality and often gave a sense of closure.

We stopped outside room 139. I placed an arm around each of the ladies shoulders and gave them a comforting hug. Mary pushed open the door. We moved to the bedside. In a circle around the bed I reached for their hands and encouraged them to join me in reciting the Lord's Prayer.

After the prayer Mary leaned over the bed and buried her face in the sheets. In a muffled, sobbing voice she spoke, *"I love you son; I forgive you."*

Suddenly, I remembered the prayer I had scribbled in the notebook when I asked Roger what he wanted me to pray for. I pulled the page from the notebook, read it, and then held it out to Carol whispering to her that this was the prayer her brother Roger had asked me to pray that morning. I suggested she read it, and then give it to her mother. Tears filled her eyes as she read: A Prayer from Roger, For My Mother, Mary. I Pray that my mother can forgive me, as I have forgiven her. I pray that she can know I love her, as I know she loves me. Your son, Roger

Carol read the prayer several times before she thrust it toward her mother. Mary wiped tears away and read the note. Miraculously, her face began to relax and grow radiant. Her eyes glistened _ not with tears _ but with a new found sense of peace.

She placed the note between her hands and positioned them in a posture of prayer in front of her face.

I breathed a *"Thank you,"* to God for answering more than one prayer that morning, and for mending a broken heart and broken relationship.

I tip toed from the room, softly closed the door, and headed down the corridor to the chaplain's office

CHAPTER 22

A Matter of Time

Tom Breslo told me that after a visit with his doctor he pulled into his driveway and turned off the engine. He said he sat for a few minutes resting his head against the steering wheel.

He tried to remember *exactly* what his family doctor had told him an hour earlier.

His thoughts went back to the doctor visit where he heard the doctor say, *"I'm sorry to have to tell you this, Tom, but all your tests came back positive. You have an inoperable brain tumor."*

Those words now pounded in his ears. He spoke his thoughts aloud. *"Now I know what's been causing my dizziness, headaches, and temporary blackouts."*

He now struggled in knowing what to do. He continued relating to me what he *had* done.

He said, *"My wife Paula met me at the door and immediately knew something was wrong. She asked,"* 'What did the doctor say?' *"I didn't know what to tell her. I went into the living room, sat on the sofa and tried to choose my words carefully. I told her, it's not good news, Honey."*

"What is it?" Paula insisted.

Tom's eyes teared as he related to me, a hospice Chaplain, how he ultimately broke

the news to his wife about his terminal illness

"As I said, I didn't know what to say. I knew I had to tell her, but I didn't know how."

"How did you finally decide?" I asked.

"I just blurted it out; I have a brain tumor!" he said. He paused to wipe tears from his eyes with his shirt sleeve and then continued, *"She fell apart. She became hysterical. It took us a week with the doctor's help for us to know what to do. Since the cancer was inoperable the doctor recommended we look at a hospice program. So here we are."*

He stopped talking, and with elbows on his knees he held his head in his hands.

I sat across from Tom and looked into his eyes as he raised his head. I could see him relax slightly. I attempted to empathize with him and enter his pool of pain.

His wife Paula had purposely avoided being present during my spiritual assessment interview with Tom. I related to her decision for wanting to be absent.

I waited a few minutes until Tom looked up and asked, *"Mr. Breslo..."* He held up his hand signaling me to stop talking and said, *"Call me Tom, Chaplain."*

I began again. *"Tom, how can I help?"*

"Well, I need a little spiritual support, Chaplain," he replied.

"Do you have a spiritual preference?" I asked.

"No. Not really. My parents called themselves Catholic but were non-practicing," he replied.

"Would you like to see a Catholic Priest?" I asked.

"No. Not really. I was baptized and confirmed, and took my first communion, but like my parents I never practiced the faith. It never had anything for me. I usually left the mass empty" he replied.

"Have you tried other churches?" I asked.

"No. I figure they are all the same," he replied.

"How can I help?" I asked again.

"Well, the doc said I didn't have long to live. That my death was just a matter of time. So I think it's appropriate to make my peace

with a Higher Power," he continued, *"Problem is, I don't know how to do that. What faith do you follow, Chaplain?"*

"I'm Christian, Non-denominational. Would you like for me to explain my belief system?" I asked.

"Yes. Yes, I would like for you to do that," he invited. It is never the intent, or purpose of a Chaplain to attempt to convert or proselytize a patient to a particular belief system. In fact, we never work from our own agenda. However, when asked, we are never forbidden to explain, or share, our own personal belief system. In fact, Tom had given permission by requesting to learn about my faith.

I spent the next forty-five minutes explaining the mainline Christendom doctrine and tenets of faith. Tom appeared to drink in my every word, and absorb it like a sponge.

I ended the explanation with a vignette on a non-religious persona experiencing a spiritual awakening and of coming to know Christ in a personal way as Savior. I concluded by asking Tom if he had any questions. He asked, *"How do I get to know Christ as my personal Savior?"*

Consistent with the doctrinal teaching of conservative, mainline Christendom, I was pleased to hold his hand, and with bowed head and closed eyes, lead him in a prayer asking God for forgiveness, and inviting Christ to come into his heart as personal Savior. *"God works in mysterious ways."*

I opened my eyes and looked at him. There appeared to be radiance about him I had not seen before. His eyes appeared to sparkle, not with tears, but a new found sense of peace.

He arose from the sofa, excitedly grabbed my hand, and said, *"Thank you, Chaplain,"* He said and embraced me in a bear hug.

I asked, *"May I come see you again?"* With a wide grin he replied, *"By all means. Please do."* I said, *"Then I'll see you, when I see you,"* turned toward the door and let myself out. Sadly, I was unable to accept his invitation. The following day, surrounded by family and friends, with peace and dignity, Tom Breslo passed from this life.

CHAPTER 23

Get Out of My Room!
Short, Not so sweet

When the patient initially came on hospice service she was very explicit about declining the spiritual component. It was reported by her family and other staff members that she was verbally abusive all of the time, and sometimes struck out at others, also becoming physically abusive.

In the health care facility, where she resided, our hospice organization had several other hospice patients with whom I, as hospice chaplain, visited routinely.

On the first visit of the New Year I asked the charge nurse about the coping welfare of the patients I was regularly seeing. She reported zero concerns. She then mentioned the patient by name who had initially declined the chaplain visits.

"Mrs. Roberts is not doing well. Would it be possible to look in on her?" she asked.

It is always the desire and intent of the hospice chaplain to respect the patient's rights to be, or not to be, seen by the chaplain. In this particular case it was *"not to be seen."*

I placed a telephone call to the R.N. managing the case. I reported that I had been requested, as Chaplain, by the charge nurse, to 'look in' on the patient. I also informed the R.N. case manager that, initially, the patient had declined to be seen by a chaplain. I was calling for input on what action to take. I suggested to the case manager that she call the family to see if permission could be obtained to see the patient, just this one time, to determine if the patient was experiencing spiritual mental angst. She agreed, made the call, whereupon, the family gave their consent to visit one time.

Having obtained family permission to visit the patient I entered her room and approached her bed. In a soft voice I introduced myself as the chaplain and addressed her by her last name.

"Mrs. Strong, I'm the Chaplain." To which she showed no response. Not knowing if she had difficulty hearing I asked. *"Did you hear me?"*

Whereupon, she replied in a loud voice, *"I heard you. What do you want?"*

"How are you getting along?" I asked.

"Not very good!" she responded again, in a louder voice.

"Who sent you here?" she asked

"Your family gave me permission to visit you," I told her. I then asked, *Can I do anything for you?" "May I pray with you while I am here?"*

Without a moment's hesitation she said, *"No, you cannot pray with me, or for me. Leave me alone! Get out of my room!"*

I thanked her for her time and exited the room. I reported the visit encounter to the charge nurse, the case manager, and the family

This was the most disappointing patient interaction of my career; *a short, not so sweet* visit.

CHAPTER 24

I Feel Cheated

I was informed about the new patient via voice mail. A thirty-five year-old Caucasian male who, two years before, had been operated on for colon cancer. According to the medical record I was reviewing, cancer was not the only life threatening illness he sustained. He was also immune system compromised. He had contracted Acquired Immune Deficiency (AIDS) 6 months earlier and had gone untreated. His name was Gene Boyd.

Mr. Boyd had agreed to be seen by the chaplain, and I had scheduled an appointment. I now stood at his door waiting for someone to answer the bell.

The door opened, I introduced myself, presented a business card, and was invited into the home.

"Don is in the bedroom" his care-giver Bob, who I learned was his significant other, stated.

I followed Bob into the darkened bedroom praying my eyes would adjust to the semi- darkness by the time I reached the patient.

I stood at the bedside and looked into the eyes of a man who appeared to be twice his biological age. He was extremely cachectic. His bones protruded through his frail body. I introduced myself.

"Hello Mr. Boyd, my name is Chaplain Curtis. Do you want me to call you Mr. Boyd, or Don?" I asked.

"Don is good," he replied, *"Everybody calls me Don. That's fine."*

"*I was pleased you made an appointment with me, Don. How can I help?*" I asked.

"*I really don't know. I just needed to talk to somebody who has some spiritual influence,*" he said.

I began the conversation by asking, "*Do you have a spiritual preference?*"

"*No. I was abandoned by my church and family when they found out I was gay,*" he said, in a sad and almost apologetic tone of voice.

"*Does your family now know you are ill?*" I continued the conversation.

"*Yeah, my brother has kept in touch, and he told my parents and grandparents. My dad is from the deep South and he is a Redneck. My mother wants to reconnect with me, but dad doesn't want anything to do with me,*" he said with voice fading.

I sensed he was becoming exhausted; I suggested that he conserve his energy and just answer my question with a yes or no reply. He quietly agreed by nodding his head.

His significant other, Bob, had left the bedroom to provide privacy for conversation between Don and myself. Don now asked me to call Bob "*for a glass of ice chips.*"

I called Bob, and told him what Don wanted. He came back with the ice chips; he came and went as quietly as a silent butler.

I resumed a limited conversation with Don. I framed my questions so as to be answered with a yes or no answer.

"*Don, would you like for me to contact a minister to come and see you?*" I asked him.

"*No. Aren't you a minister?*" he asked.

"*Yes, I am a minister,*" I replied.

"*You'll do,*" he said with a faint smile.

"*Good. I'll be pleased to be your pastor, if you want me to be,*" I assured him. He nodded agreement.

"*Would you want me to talk with your parents, Don,*" I asked.

"*Yes. And my sister. My sister has kids I have never met. I feel cheated,*" he said with a forlorn look.

I told him I would do what I could to help reconcile and re-connect the family members with him. I also told him to think about what could help from a spiritual perspective, He agreed that he would. He appeared to be very pleased. I asked if he wanted me to pray with him before I left. He consented to prayer.

During our visit Don appeared to have gained a burst of energy and was excited about the prospect of reconciling with family members.

Over the next several months I was able to speak with his parents, his sister, and brother, who had stayed in touch with him. We were pleased to later learn of reconciliation and first time visits with estranged nieces and nephews.

In the sixth month of his illness _ although I had been seeing him regularly _ he called my office and requested a visit. I again stood in his bedroom by his hospital bed.

If possible, he appeared to have lost a remarkable amount of weight since my last visit a week before. His body literally appeared to be skin and bone. His limp, weak, handshake further evidenced his decreased energy and strength. His voice however, was strong.

"Chaplain, you have explained your religious faith of Christianity to me and I liked what I heard. I know I don't have too much longer to live, so I want to prepare to meet my Maker.

As much as I want to live, I'm ready to prepare to meet God. I am so thankful to you for all the help you have given me in assisting to reconcile my family, and especially, the opportunity to meet my nieces and nephews."

I was pleased to pray with Don and lead him in a prayer of reconciliation with God in asking for forgiveness.

As I prepared to leave, Don grasped my hand again with unbelievable strength for his weakened condition. Tears slid down his cheeks as he said, *"If I don't see you again here on earth, I'll see you one day in Heaven. Thank you for all you've done; thank you for everything."*

He kissed my hand and said, *"You have been a good pastor."*

I asked if he would like some prayers; he replied, *"Yes. Please."*

I offered prayer, ending with the Our Father prayer, gave him a blessing and anointed him with oil. When I said to him *"Bye for now"* He appeared to be remarkably at peace.

I sensed that this would be my final visit with him; it was. Don passed away at 4:45 A.M. December 25th; Christmas day.

CHAPTER 25

I Think I'm Feeling My Old Age

I arrived at the assisted living health care facility to see a 101 year-old male patient who had been diagnosed with a terminal illness. He had been placed in the hospice care program with a company for whom I serve as a Chaplain.

His name was John Kaplan. His family had requested the spiritual component for the patient. My visit was to complete a spiritual assessment to determine the patient's spiritual needs.

I met Mr. Kaplan in the multi-purpose activity room where he sat with other residents watching television. I introduced myself, to which he extended his hand in greeting. To begin establishing rapport with him I jokingly asked, *"What is your secret for living to 101 years of age?"*

He looked me in the eye with an alert and pleasant affect and replied, *"By just being a descent human being."*

He continued to look at me and, with a twinkle in his eyes said, *"And you might try shaving once in a while,"* and broke into a laugh. I joined in his laughter because I wear a full beard.

We continued our conversation. I asked, *"Do you have a belief system?"*

"I'm Lutheran," he replied

"Would you like to see a Lutheran minister?" I asked.

"His answer was an emphatic *"No!"*

I again reminded him that I was a clergyman and asked, *"Will I do, to provide you with spiritual support?"*

"I guess so," he replied.

Mr. Kaplan had a good sense of humor and we enjoyed a pleasant and productive visit. I concluded the visit by asking if I could say a prayer with him, and he agreed. Before praying I asked if I may come see him again. *"Any time, Chaplain, any time,"* he invited.

Two weeks later, on my next visit, I again met Mr. Kaplan in the multi-purpose activity room. He had been watching TV and had dozed off. He appeared to be comfortably slumped over in a relaxed position in a rocker recliner chair.

He aroused to the sound of my voice as I softly spoke his name, *"Good afternoon, Mr. Kaplan."*

He opened his eyes, yawned, and said, *"Well, hello!"*

I asked, *"How are you getting along?"*

He winched as he adjusted his posture in the chair. I sensed that he might be in pain. I asked do you *"Hurt anywhere?"*

"No," he replied, *"I think I'm just feeling my old age,"* and laughed out loud.

I joined in his laughter and jokingly remarked, *"I don't know why you would be feeling your old age; you are only 101 years old!"*

He again laughed aloud and said, *"You're all right. I like you."*

Mr. Kaplan's daughter, who was a retired Registered Nurse, had told him, the doctor said he had only 3 to 6 months to live when he became a hospice patient.

In fact, Mr. Kaplan lived for another 7 months and 2 days. He passed from this life Thursday, November 21st on his birthday at age 102.

CHAPTER 26

He Can't Be Dead!

Ringing of the phone awakened me at 4:30 P.M.; I was on call. You know, when the phone rings at 4:30 A.M., it can't be *good* news. I answered and recognized the voice of the on call nurse. She said, *"Chaplain, Mr. Gonzales just expired and there are about twenty-five family members here.*

Two daughters are clinging to their father and are refusing to accept his death saying, 'He can't be dead!' I think it would be of great help to the daughters and rest of the family if you could come."

I assured her that I would, and asked her to tell the family. I was not familiar with the patient by name. I pulled up the patient information from the on call book. It stated that the patient was 57 years-old, and that he had a diagnosis of cirrhosis of the liver, alcohol related. I gave the nurse an approximate time of arrival and asked her to stay with the family until I arrived.

The distance to the patient's home _ according to the Map Quest _ was approximately 35 miles. Being unfamiliar with the area I knew it would take just under an hour to reach the area of the patient's home.

The sun was setting on the Western horizon when I pulled into the driveway. I noted several people were standing around outside the house smoking and waiting for my arrival. The nurse came out of the house to meet me, bring me up to date, and to take me to the family for introductions.

She told me that the daughters were still clinging to their father and sobbing over their loss. The rest of the family members appeared to be accepting and coping more appropriately.

The nurse led me into the home. I was directed to the living room. A hospital bed had been placed in the center of the room and the daughters sat on either side of the father's bed softly crying with muffled sobs. I offered a hand to each and expressed my condolence.

The daughters explained that their father was Catholic and had been seen in the hospital by a Priest for sacraments and the anointing of the sick (formerly called the Last Rites).

The patient had deteriorated rapidly and had expired within one week after being discharged from the hospital and placed on hospice service.

By now, all of the family members had returned to the home and were silently standing around the room. I asked how I could help.

The patient's wife, Yolanda, spoke to me in broken English, *"Father, please say prayers for Him..."*

I told the family what I was going to do: "Read from the Psalms, say prayers, have the family gather around the bed encircling it, join hand and recite with me the Our Father Prayer. I explained that them, I would be available to any family member who would like to speak with me privately."

All of the family members, including the two daughters who had calmed down considerably, appeared to be pleased, and in agreement, with what I had explained that I was going to do.

The spiritual dynamics were facilitated and completed just prior to the mortuary arriving for removal of the body and transporting to the mortuary of choice.

I stayed, along with the on call nurse, until the body was removed. The family told us that funeral arrangements had already been made with a local Catholic memorial park and cemetery.

I informed the family I would remain available to any and all family members if there was a continuing need. I gave everyone a collective blessing of, "God be with you," prior to leaving.

There appeared to be a sense of acceptance, with normal bereavement, grief, sadness and tears. No high risk family members were identified. Each member thanked me and seemed to be coping appropriately at the time of my leaving.

CHAPTER 27

Why Did This Happen?

A shrill ringing awakened me from a sound sleep. At first, I didn't know if it was the Telephone, or the alarm. The second ring left no doubt. I picked up the receiver and spoke into the mouthpiece.

"*Hello, this is Chaplain Curtis speaking*" I said.

"*Hello Chaplain Curtis...*" a tear filled voice spilled into my ear. Chaplain, Ray is in the hospital. I recognized the voice of one of my church members. I responded to her pain filled plea.

"*Betty,*" I said softly, trying to calm her down, "*tell me what has happened,*" I encouraged her reply.

"*Ray couldn't breathe, and I called 911. They took him to the hospital emergency room, and admitted him,*" she told me.

I remembered about her telling me about another time Ray had been hospitalized for congestive heart failure (CHF), and shortness of breath (SOB). Her words came back to me.

The doctor had told him that he was prone to having cirrhosis of the live alcohol related.

He had told him that he needed to stop drinking, lose weight, exercise, and take care of himself.

Ray had failed to follow his doctor's advice. Now he was suffering the consequences; in the hospital again with the same problem.

"*I will be at the hospital as soon as possible and that I would meet her there*" I told Betty. When I arrived Ray was hooked up in both arms with lines leading to IVAC pumps. He was semi-comatose and verbally non-responsive. I was informed by Betty that the doctors were unsure about his condition and were struggling in knowing how to make a definitive diagnoses.

"They are continuing to run tests to determine what's wrong," She told me.

Not so consequently, Ray had made a profession of faith in Christ as personal Savior approximately one year earlier when my wife and I had visited with them in their home. I reminded Betty of this occasion. She appeared to relax a little and to have more peace of mind as she, too, recalled the incident.

I stayed with Betty and Ray at the hospital for approximately an hour, read scripture, said prayers, blessed and anointed Ray. Before I left, I told her I *"was a close as your phone, and to call me if there was any change in Ray's condition."* She nodded and said. *"I will."*

The next day I heard from Betty. *"Pastor, Ray has been diagnosed with cirrhosis of the liver and is not expected to live more than six months. His doctor said he is 'hospice appropriate.' Oh, Pastor, how did this happen?"* Betty asked in a pain-filled voice, and broke into tears.

I assisted Betty with her decision to place Ray in a hospice program. She choose the hospice agency where I serve as chaplain. As her pastor, and now their chaplain, I continued to provide on-going spiritual support to both Ray, Betty and the family members.

Subsequently, following his admission to hospice, Ray appeared to have a burst of energy, and became quasi verbally responsive. He remained on medication, for extreme pain, administered by IV's and IVAC pump dispensers.

Ultimately, Ray was discharged from the acute care hospital and transferred to a skilled nursing facility (SNF) for comfort and palliative care. I continued to see him and wife Betty for spiritual and emotional support. Most of the times I would see him he was non-responsive.

Three weeks after the on-set of Ray's terminal diagnosis, and hospice care, I received a telephone call from Betty. She informed me, *"Ray passed away this morning at 3:45 A.M."* I looked at my watch. It read 730 A.M. I asked her where she was.

"I'm still at the health care facility," she told me.

I drove to the facility and assisted her in making arrangement for removal of the remains and funeral plans with a local cemetery and mortuary for the memorial service.

I later learned that Ray experienced a peaceful death. This knowledge helped Betty to cope more appropriately with the loss of her soul mate of 37 years.

Four days later, I considered it a privilege and honor, when I was requested by Betty and the family, to officiate the funeral memorial service.

CHAPTER 28

It Hasn't Sunk in Yet

He extended his hand in greeting and said, *"It's good to see you, Chaplain."*

"Thank you for agreeing to see me," I replied shaking his hand.

"How are you getting along?" I asked.

"Oh, pretty good, I guess, I'm just tired," he answered.

Sam Newhouse had been diagnosed with liver cancer three months prior to my visit.

Tiredness and lethargy were signs and symptoms of his life limiting illness. According to his medical chart he had lost thirty pounds since his diagnosis.

After some small talk, I turned the conversation to the reason for which I came; to complete a spiritual assessment as to any spiritual needs which needed to be addressed.

"What did your doctor tell you?" I asked.

"He told me I have a terminal illness and there is nothing that they can do for me," he replied.

"What does that mean to you," I queried.

"Well, it means that I am dying, that I don't have too much longer to live," he told me.

"How are you processing that information?" I asked.

"I'm not. It hasn't sunk in yet. I'm finding it very difficult to believe. I'm 53 years old.

I've never been sick a day in my life. Suddenly I am told I have liver cancer. I am finding it difficult to accept," he said.

"Are you frightened?" I asked.

"Frightened? Scared is a better word. I just don't know what to expect. I don't know about the unknown," he continued.

"Do you want to talk about it?" I inquired.

"I don't know how to talk about the terminal illness. I don't feel sick. I just feel tired with very little energy," he informed me.

"Are you a religious person?" I asked.

"No. Not really. My parents were Jewish. I never went through a Bar Mitzvah, I just wasn't interested. They never tried to force me. They always said religion had to be my choice," he said, and continued, *"Sometimes I watch evangelistic programs on Channel 40, "* (a local Praise the Lord Television Channel).

"Would you like for me to facilitate a Rabbi to come and see you and talk with you?" I asked.

"No. It wouldn't do any good. They wouldn't be able to help me," he answered.

"What about a Christian minister? Would you want to talk with a pastor?" I asked.

"No. I don't think so. Why can't I talk with you? You're a minister, aren't you?" he asked.

"Yes. I am a Christian minister, a pastor as well as a chaplain for hospice. I'll be pleased to talk with you and answer any questions I can. What would you like to talk about?" I asked..

"What's this born again experience I hear them talking about on TV?" he asked.

"In Christian circles that's what they call a 'Spiritual Awakening,'" I told him.

"What does that mean?" he asked.

"Well, in order for you to fully understand it, I will have to explain to you the Christian doctrine," I answered, and continued, *"Would you like for me to explain that?"*

"Do you have the time?" he asked.

"Sure. I'll take the time, Mr. Newhouse," I told him.

He held up his hand and said, *"Whoa! My dad's name was Mr. Newhouse; Call me Sam.*

I explained the traditional, conservative, evangelical view based on the Gospel of John and the visit by the Jewish Sanhedrin Judge Nicodemus to Jesus, and how Jesus compared physical death to the natural, or *first* birth, to the spiritual birth, or *"new birth"* or *second* (eternal)birth.

I concluded with the evangelical position concerning birth, life, death and eternity. That is, a person is born *one time* in the natural *physical birth*, and eventually dies a *physical death*. If that person dies a physical death, without experiencing the "new," *spiritual* birth (having a Spiritual Awakening), or "born again experience," then, according to the teaching of the scriptures, their soul will be "lost" or "unsaved."

Thus, without the spiritual birth, a person has *one birth, and two death; physical and eternal.* However, according to the teaching of scripture, and the evangelical faith, for a person who has a spiritual awakening experience, that is, a "new birth," or "born again experience," by coming to know Christ in a personal way through personal invitation to Christ, to come into the heart and forgive that persons sins, and become their Savior, then that person will experience not only a natural birth, but a spiritual birth, or "born again experience," as well. Thus, *two births, physical and spiritual, and only one physical death.*

I paused and asked,*" Do you understand the spiritual dynamics I have explained? Do you have any questions?"*

Tom Newhouse had listened intently to the explanation of what is the "new birth experience" _ according to the teachings of the scriptures and the fundamental evangelicals' interpretation _ of the New Testament Gospel of John.

Finally he answered, *"Yes. I understand. It sounds so simple. What do I have to do, to receive this new birth?"* he asked.

I reiterated the conservative, fundamental, doctrinal and

theological position; to ask Christ for forgiveness of his sins, and invite Christ into his heart to become his personal Savior and Lord and Master of his life. With a Spiritual Awakening he committed his life to Christ.

Wednesday, a week after our visit, he slipped into a comma. Sam Newhouse never came out of the comma. Thursday morning, at 4:10 A.M., surrounded by family and friends, with dignity and peace of mind, Sam Newhouse slid into a comma and never awakened.

CHAPTER 29

My Buddy!

I received a message from my office to call Patricia Gordon. The name was familiar but I couldn't place it. I wrote down the number and placed the call.

A female voice said, *"Hello. Who is this?"* The voice sounded vaguely familiar

"Patricia, this is Curtis. I'm returning your call," I said.

"Curtis, do you remember me?" she asked

Her voice had a British accent. I racked my brain trying to remember the voice; memories came flooding back.

Before I could answer she said, *"I now have brain cancer."*

As she spoke, I placed her. She had been a hospice patient approximately four years ago with the hospice agency where I serve as Chaplain, and she had been my patient.

"Patricia, I do remember you. How could I ever forget you? We had many wonderful chats," I reminded her.

"Yes, I remember well that's why I'm calling" she replied.

"I'm sorry you have brain cancer," I told her, and continued, *"Are you coming back on hospice?"*

"No, not yet," she said, *"But what I wanted to ask you is, would you still officiate my funeral service?"* she asked.

"I would consider it an honor," I told her.

"Good," she said, *"I'm going to make a note of it for my son."*

I assured her I would know, when she came back on service with the hospice program and would again be pleased to be her chaplain for spiritual support. She thanked me. We chatted a few more minutes, bade each other good bye, and said our good byes..

Approximately six months passed and the incident had slipped from my mind. A three day holiday week-end Saturday, Sunday, Monday came up, wherein I returned to work on Tuesday. I reviewed the census and the new patients who had been assigned to me, and I recognized Patricia Gordon's name. She had been admitted to the hospice program the previous Friday at which time she was alert and oriented, aware and responsive. I hastened to contact her and called her home.

I was expecting to hear Patricia's voice. Instead, her son Shaun answered. I had never met Shaun, but I knew who he was, through my conversations with Patricia. He also knew who I was. I introduced myself and told him the reason for the call. There was silence for a few minutes and then I heard his voice again.

"Chaplain," he began, *"I found a note my mother left on her nightstand. Let me read it to you."*

He read, *"Dear Shawny, when the time is right, I want you to call Chaplain Curtis Smith, Ph.D. He is my buddy."*

I thanked him for the information he had shared from the note and told him I wanted to make an appointment to Patricia.

"She's out of it, Chaplain," he told me.

"That's O.K." I assured him, *"I still want to come and say some prayers for her."*

"Sure, Chaplain, you're welcome to come," he invited. I told him *"I will be there in about an hour."*

I arrived to find him standing on the sidewalk waiting for me. We greeted each other, after which he invited me into the house. After some small talk he steered me into the bedroom where Patricia lay on her side using oxygen continuously. I knelt by the bedside and spoke into her ear, *Patricia, it's Chaplain Curtis,"* I said, She moved her head and turned onto her back.

With closed eyes, she took my hand as I placed it in her hand. I said to her, *"Squeeze my hand if you can hear me."* With a strong grip she squeezed my hand. I knew she was hearing what I was saying.

I said, *"How good it is to see you again,"* She squeezed my hand again.

I told her, *"I am going to say some prayers for you, give you a blessing and an anointing."*

I asked her, *"Will that be O.K.?"* I again felt a hand squeeze, much weaker this time.

While holding her hand, I said a prayer into her ear. I then gave her a blessing and anointed her with oil.

I told her, *"I love you in the Lord."* Then I whispered into her ear, *"If I don't see you again here on planet earth, I will see you in Heaven one day."*

For the last time, I again felt a faint squeeze of my hand. I invoked God's blessing of, *"God be with you,"* and left the bedroom, to learn that the family had been standing outside the doorway, observing my intervention with Patricia. They smiled, nodded approval and appreciation.

I assured son Shaun that *"I am as close as your phone,"* and encouraged him to call at any time. I glanced at my watch as I left the home: it read 5:15 P.M.

I received notice that, surrounded by her family, Patricia passed from this life that evening at 6:45 P.M.

The next several days I waited for a call from Shaun regarding the funeral service. I had previously told him I would be available at his convenience. On a Wednesday following Patricia's death I did receive a call.

"I would like a home memorial service with just a few relatives and friends present," he said. He requested a visit from me at his home the following day.

I arrived and was welcomed into the home. I had the privilege of meeting Shaun's wife Betty, for the first time. I was told that a memorial folder had already been prepared by Betty to include a beautifully written tribute, touching on the highlights of Patricia's life; a touching wonderful tribute.

It appeared as if most of the memorial work had already been accomplished. I would simply have to coordinate the order of service. This was a plus for me. Because of my closeness to Patricia we appeared to have formed a bond, and, from an emotional perspective, I would have struggled to present an unemotional eulogy.

More people arrived at the home for the memorial than had been expected. Nineteen had been expected; approximately 30 appeared. Soon it was time to begin the service. Amidst favorite music from classical, to western, prayers, scripture reading, and spoken tributes, the order of service progressed and ended with the Our Father prayer, and a blessing of the people.

The *"Rule of Thumb"* for health care professionals' cautions *'do not get emotionally connected or involved with your patients,'* I had violated that caution. I had lost a good friend who called me *'My Buddy:'* God *called* her home.

CHAPTER 30

I'm Nothing

With a change in chaplains, this was my first visit with an 81 year-old female patient who had been diagnosed with Paralysis Agitans (Parkinson's Disease). Having called the home I had spoke with the 24 hour primary care giver, Clarice, who stated, *"She's eating right now. Can you call back?"* she asked.

"Yes. When should I call back?" I asked.

"Call back in about an hour," she instructed me.

"O.K.," I said. The dial tone spilled into my ear.

I called back, approximately and hour later and again spoke with Clarice.

"Is Mrs. August through eating?" I asked

"Yes," she replied.

"Would she want a visit from the chaplain today?" I asked.

"Let me ask her," she said.

"Take your time," I said, cooperating with her.

Her voice came back on the phone, *"She said its O.K. to visit right away, and to make it a short visit."*

"O.K., I'll be there soon; thirty minutes or less," I said accepting the invitation.

I arrived at the home and introduced myself to the care giver Clarice who answered the door.

"I'm Chaplain Curtis," I said. She opened wide the door, invited me in, and said, *"Mrs. August is in the living room."*

I walked through the entrance. Clarice pointed toward the living room. I observed a frail looking, light-complexioned woman sitting on the sofa. She smiled as I approached, and extended her hand in a limp handshake.

I introduced myself and told her I was her newly assigned spiritual counselor.

"What happened to the other one?" she asked.

I informed her, *"He retired,"*

I sat on a straight-backed chair, which Clarice had moved alongside the sofa for me. I cautiously opened the conversation.

"I understand you are a Protestant," I said.

"If that what it says in my records, then that is wrong. I am nothing; absolutely nothing" she replied with emphasis.

"Oh, your records do not identify your belief system," I assured her, and continued, *"I was simply under that impression,"*

"The only time I ever attended church was when I went with a friend who invited me, but I never joined or connected" she said. *"My friends have tried to make me a Baptist, Catholic, Lutheran, and Methodist, but it didn't work. I am still nothing."*

She used the term *almost* as if she was *proud,* from a spiritual perspective, to be *'nothing'.*

Of course, right away, I recognized what she was trying to say. That she had no spiritual affinity.

"Do you have a belief system?" I asked.

"I really don't have a belief system," she told me.

"Well, you really do," I said with a smile. *"Not to have a belief system, is to have a belief system."*

"I guess I never looked at it like that," she said, returning my smile.

"Is there anything you need to talk about today, Mrs. August?" I asked.

"What did you have in mind," she asked.

"You agenda is my agenda," I assured her.

"Not that I can think of," she replied.

"Any open or unresolved issues?" I asked.

"There may be one," she answered.

"Do you want to talk about it?" I encouraged.

"It's about my brother. He and I are not talking; we haven't spoken to one another in twenty years, " she said in an agonizing, sad voice.

"What do you want to do about that?" I asked.

"I don't know," she honestly answered.

"Do you want to reconcile?" I asked.

"I'd like to," she said, *"but to tell you the truth, I don't even know why we stopped talking to each other."*

"Do you know where he is? How to locate him? " I asked.

"He's in the San Francisco area I think. I have another brother who has stayed in contact with him. He knows where he is. It wouldn't be hard locating him," she told me.

"Good, then you would be able to communicate with him," I said.

"Yeah, I guess so, if I decide to," she replied.

"Didn't you say you would like to reconcile?" I asked, remembering her previous statement.

"Yes. I did say that. But what could I say? I wouldn't know what to talk about," she said.

"Well, if you really want to communicate, and reconcile, I could help you write a letter," told her.

"You would do that?" she asked, in honest disbelief.

"Yes. I would be pleased to help you write a letter using your own words," I told her.

"I want to think about it," she advised me.

"Good. It's important for you to think about it, before you make a decision," I said, agreeing with her.

On follow-up visits, we again talked about religiosity, and the fact that Mrs. August was *"nothing,"* (her word), as far as her own spirituality was concerned. It appeared to be a light and humorous subject, at least in discussions with her.

On one of my last visits, before she passed, the subject of reconciliation with her estranged brother came up again.

"Chaplain, I've had time to think about my brother Edward with whom I am alienated. I've decided I do want to reconcile. But there could be a problem. What if he never answers my letter? I would feel even worse than I feel now," she pondered her decision.

"I can tell you have given this a lot of thought, Mrs. August. You have a good question.

"Please let me try to explain the dynamics. First of all, with your letter you will have made an honest effort to restore the broken relationship with your brother. "Obviously, you will have taken time and opportunity to express yourself, your love, and your feelings, and will have apologized and asked for forgiveness for anything you did, even though you didn't then, and do not now, know the reason, for the broken relationship.

"Having done all this in your letter, you will have empowered and enabled your brother to respond to you. If he chooses not to respond, it is not your problem; it is his problem.

"Realistically, you will have emptied yourself, and by the effort you have made, you will be blameless with a clear conscious,

"It is important not to try and anticipate your brother's reaction, or lack of action, to your overture. Just know, that you can only be responsible for your own actions," I suggested to her.

"That makes a lot of sense," she said, and agreed with my reasoning. At the following visits the brother was located, the letter was written, and the reconciliation was made.

Mr. August wrote back within the week of receiving her letter. She shared his comments:

"Dear Sis, thank you for your letter. Yes, I, too, want to reconcile with you. For your information, neither do I know, or remember, the reason for our stopping talking. But whatever it is, or was, is unimportant now. I, too, want to mend our broken relationship. I

apologize to you, and ask your forgiveness for anything I have done, or failed to do, in relation to our sibling rivalry. Please accept my apology and forgive me. Please call me on the phone so we can talk in person. I plan to come to southern California in November. I will make it a point to plan to see you and spend some time with you. In the meantime, let's catch up on twenty years via telephone, letter and Email.

Thank you for caring for me, and loving me enough to take the time and effort to reconnect. I love you. Your brother Edward."

She stopped reading and folded the letter. Tears slid down her cheeks.

"Thank you, Chaplain," she said. *"For helping me reconcile and make up with my brother, Edward. Now, I can die in peace."*

It's unknown as to whether Mrs. August ever reconciled with a Higher Power. Neither do we do know what emotions stirred her mind and heart from a spiritual perspective. But we do know that, in her own words, she did, *"die in peace."*

CHAPTER 31

Age is a Blessing; a Rite of Passage

I first met John Washington, a 99 year-old, African American male, when he came on service, as a hospice patient with a terminal diagnosis of Congestive Heart Failure (CHF), in March, at a health care facility where he had been living for several years.

I made arrangements to visit with him, for a spiritual assessment, with regard to his spiritual needs.

We appeared to gain instant rapport. I learned that he was a very religious person, and had a healthy respect for clergy. As we chatted, I soon discovered that he was alert, oriented and exceptionally clear headed, with a sharp, long-term memory.

His bright, grey eyes seemed to sparkle when he spoke of his past. Over time he told me about his career as a chauffeur to a wealthy family in the state of Georgia.

His face would light up as he recounted how, each year in winter time, he would drive the family in their limo, from Georgia to their home in Florida. He beamed as he talked about his driving record; *"...over 200,000 miles, in a 15 year period, without an accident. Not even a fender bender,"* he said with a laugh.

Our friendship grew with each visit. I remember on a St. Patrick's holiday I met Johnny (he insisted I call him that), in the activities room where he sat in a wheel chair with other residents, at the assisted living health care facility where he resided. There was a pianist present and the residents joined their voices in singing good old Irish songs such as, *"My Sweet Irish Rose;" "When Irish Eyes Are Smiling,"* and other, appropriate Irish song and jigs.

The pianist suddenly stopped playing and announced: *"Johnny will now sing Danny Boy."*

With the pianist accompanying him, I listened attentively as Johnny began to sing, in a rich Baritone voice. From memory, he sang all the lyrics. When he finished singing the other residents gave him a resounding ovation of applause.

I said to him, *"You did a great job, Johnny."*

He smiled and said, *"I love to sing to music."*

I later learned that not only did he *"love to sing to music,"* he loved to sing, *period.*

I recall, on another visit, meeting him in the TV activity room where he sat alone in a wheel chair. When I approached he was singing.

"What are you singing, Johnny?" I asked.

"The resurrection song about my Lord," he replied.

"Don't stop," I said, *"please continue singing to me."*

Again, in a rich, baritone he sang all verse of the resurrection song, *"Were You There When They Crucified My Lord?"*

On another occasion, he told me about how his parents had been *"slaves on a plantation."* How, *"in spite of slavery, their 'Master' was considerate and kind, and treated them with respect."* It is uncertain as to whether he was remembering the actual reality of treatment, or through the eyes of compassionate spirituality. In any event, it was obvious, that his character had been formed with an attitude of gratitude, and that, he had been reared, at the knee of loving parents who were deeply religious.

Beyond his solid religious convictions, and genuine caring demeanor, three distinct physical characteristics were apparent:

At 99 years of age he did not need glasses. His hearing was unimpaired, and he had all of his own teeth! Johnny did not view these unique characteristics as "unique" to him. He simply said, *"God has been good; he has blessed me."*

Johnny had always told me, *"I'm going to live until my 100th birthday. After that, God can take me home."*

On September 6th Johnny celebrated his 100th birthday. A gala party was held for him, planned by the activity director and staff, in the dining room of the health care facility. As Chaplain, I was invited to attend the party. He was loudly applauded, after which, everyone sang the *Happy Birthday* song.

The candles were lighted, all ten of them, (one for every 10 years), and then were easily blown out by Johnny. The cake was cut, ice cream added, and joyfully eaten by all. With moist eyes Johnny thanked everyone for their *"generous recognition."*

Johnny then sang an old Negro Spiritual Hymn, *"Nearer My God to Thee."*

On that same occasion, Johnny told me, *"Well, Chaplain, God can take me home any time now. I had sort of asked him to let me see my 100th birthday, and he did."*

Of the many hospice patients I have ministered to, Johnny had brought one of the greatest blessings to my life, and work. His many years was exceeded only by his immeasurable faith in a Divine Power; a faith that had never failed him.

God must have wanted to receive some of the blessings *only* Johnny *could* bring. On September 13th one week after celebrating his 100th birthday, God called Johnny home.

CHAPTER 32

I've Made My Peace With God

The hospice case manager suggested I see a 67 year-old hospice patient who had been diagnosed with liver cancer and admitted to the hospice program. It had been his request *"to see the Chaplain,"* for spiritual support.

Entering the patient's room my eyes were drawn to a slight built, dark complexioned man who displayed a neatly trimmed, black moustache. His eyes were closed and he appeared to be sleeping. I called his name and he aroused to the sound of my voice.

"Hello, Mr. Rivera," I greeted him, *"My name is Curtis and I am the hospice chaplain."*

"Oh," he replied, *"I asked the nurse to call you."*

"Yes. I received your message. That's why I'm here. How can I help?" I asked.

"I'm Catholic, and I wanted you to pray for me," he said.

"Good. Do you have any special requests?" I asked trying to determine his spiritual need.

"Yes. I want you to pray for my family," he told me.

"Sure, it will be my pleasure to pray for you, and for them," I assured him.

"Can we talk before we pray?" I asked.

"Yes," he said, giving me permission.

Mr. Rivera, how are you feeling?" I asked.

"I'm O.K., I guess. I could be better," he replied.

"What is wrong with you; what did your doctor tell you?" I continued to probe around to find answers that would assist me in my prayers.

"My doctor said I have cancer," he replied without a moment's hesitation.

"What does that mean to you?" I asked, trying to establish his level of acceptance.

"It means I don't have long to live; I'm going to die," he replied.

"How are you dealing with that?" I asked.

"With eyes brimming with tears he said, *"Chaplain, we are all going to die. Nobody escapes death.*

"Would you like for me to facilitate a Priest to come and see you for sacraments?" I asked.

"No. That's O.K.," he said, *"I have made my peace with God."*

"Wonderful," I said, agreeing with his decision.

At his request, I said some prayers for him, and his family members, and asked him to join in reciting the Our Father prayer.

Sensing his energy and strength were weakening I prepared to leave.

"May I come see you again?" I asked.

"Any time, Chaplain; any time," he invited.

I told him, *"I will see you again in a week or so,"* invoked God's blessing of, *"God be with you,"* and left the home.

On a follow up, visit Mr. Rivera appeared to be coping more appropriately. I greeted him. *"Hello, Mr. Rivera,"* he extended his hand, and I extended mine in mutual greeting.

I asked how he was getting along, and if he was in any pain.

He replied, *"Not too good, Chaplain. No, I'm not in pain. I just don't feel very good."*

"What can I do for you to make you feel better? Do you want me to pray for you?" I asked.

He looked at me, smiled and said, *"No. I don't feel that bad!"*

We both had a good belly laugh. I shook his hand, and told him, *"I will see you when I see you."* He replied, *"Don't wait too long. I really do feel better after your visits;"* the feeling was mutual.

CHAPTER 33

No open Issues Except...

The 65 year-old patient Ramona Salvador lay on her back in a hospital bed which had been placed in a corner of her living room.

She had requested to see a Chaplain at the time she had been admitted to the hospice program. She was assigned to me. My purpose in seeing her today was to complete a Spiritual Assessment as to her spiritual needs. My visit was in response to her request. Aside from obtaining information, with regard to her spiritual needs, as with all hospice team members, I was expected to assess her level of comfort, especially insofar as pain was concerned.

I asked her, *"Do you have any pain today?"* to which she replied in broken English.

"*No, Senior, no delore*" (Spanish for pain).

"Good," I said, and continued my assessment, *"How are you getting along?"*

"*Asi, asi, Padre,*" she replied,(Spanish for so, so).

It appeared that her understanding of the English language was better than her speaking of it. She was able to follow my voice and answer my questions remarkably well. Ramona's daughter, Mary, who was bilingual and spoke English fluently, stood close by to interpret if language became a barrier in our communication.

"What did your doctor tell you, Ramona?" I asked.

She informed me that her doctor said *"Breast cancer, with only 6 months to live."*

She went on to say that she was Catholic, and her faith was keeping her going. *"My parish Priest is visiting me regularly for holy communion and prayers."* She said from a spiritual perspective she was doing," *Muy bien,"* (Spanish, for very good).

I was nearing the end of my limited Spanish speaking, so daughter Mary translated for us.

I have to admit, with translation, the spiritual assessment interview was going much smoother. Part of the information I tried to learn from Ramona was, if she was in any distress or pain.

As our conversation and discussion progressed, I asked Ramona if there was any unfinished business, or open issues.

She thought for a few minutes and then said, *"No, Senior, I don't think so,"* then suddenly, she remembered something.

She explained, through translation, that the home she lived in was one of four, on her property, which she owned. Three were rentals. She hesitated for a moment then continued, *"I haven't paid income tax for two years, and I'm worried."*

She asked me to pray for her that she *"Wouldn't get into trouble with the government."*

I was pleased to pray with her, after which I assured her, she would not have to worry about *'get(ting) into trouble with the government.'* Now, obviously, the income from the property would have to be reported, and taxes paid by her survivors. However, to set her mind at ease, I felt it wise to assure her that she *personally*, would not have to be concerned with the issue.

I encouraged her to live one day at a time, and to get the most out of the life she was blessed with, for however long, or short, the remaining time was.

"She said, *"Si Senior. Gracias."*

She asked me to pray that *"God will take me home."*

As it turned out, Ramona didn't have to worry about *'not having paid income tax for two years.'* And the prayer I prayed was *not* for

'*God to take her home.*' Rather, "*that God will grant unto you the desire of your heart.*"

Eleven days later, God answered *that* prayer and did "*grant unto her the desire of her heart;*" he took her home.

CHAPTER 34

When it's Time...

The 83 year-old female hospice patient extended her hand in greeting when I introduced myself. *"I'm Annie Gabriel,"* she said. She had recently been discharged from the hospital, and diagnosed with end stage uterine cancer. Lying on the couch in the living room, she appeared weak and lethargic

With her permission, I was in her home by appointment, for a Spiritual Assessment, to determine any spiritual needs. She assured me that she was receiving strong support from her own pastor who had visited her in the hospital, and had visited twice already in her home since her discharge from the hospital."

"My pastor is very attentive," she said, *"But I am very pleased you have come to visit."*

As the visit progressed, so did the rapport. She began to open up.

"When I received my terminal diagnosis, Chaplain, I told the family I did not want any chemo or radiation therapy treatments. I did not want to be any sicker than I already am."

She continued to open up to me. Mrs. Gabriel share how she had been widowed eleven months ago. When she and her husband Ben *"returned home from eating dinner at a local restaurant."* She related how *"Ben complained of mild chest pain and decided to go to bed early.*

She went on to say, *"The next morning he was gone. Now, I will soon be with him in Heaven."*

Her eyes became moist as she spoke, and a tear slid down her cheek. She continued to talk, *"I want to die. I have been very unhappy since I lost Ben. He was my life. I'm not even happy anymore with my family. My grandson is getting married next week and I won't be going."* Is that because you don't feel well, Mrs. Gabriel?" I asked.

"No. I just won't be going," she replied

"You will be able to see a video," I empathized with her.

"Yeah, I guess so. They probably will have a video taken," she said. She didn't sound too excited.

We continued to talk about her illness, her grandson, a granddaughter, both of whom she was very pleased with and, her wish to die.

Not wanting to tire her, I began to bring my visit to a close. *"Thank you for seeing me today, Mrs. Gabriel. May I come see you again?"*

"Yes, if I'm still around," she answered, alluding to the fact that she might not be living when I attempted to visit her again.

"May I pray with you before I go?" I asked.

"Yes. But don't pray that I will get better. I really want to die, and wish I could," she said.

I prayed, *"God grant unto Mrs. Gabriel the desire of her heart, and give her peace,"* She seemed to be pleased with the prayer and said, *"Thank you, Chaplain."*

Less than two weeks later, one week before her 84th birthday, consistent with her request, Mrs. Annie Gabriel went to be with her husband and life mate Ben.

God heard and answered her prayer, and granted her the desire of her heart; her wish of *"I really want to die, and wish I could."*

CHAPTER 35

I've Been Laid Off...

I had been assigned to a new patient who was being transferred from a private residence to a board and care facility. The patient's behavior had become unmanageable for the son, his wife and their adult children. Subsequently, there was a caregiver crisis.

The patient was an 87 year-old Hispanic male who had been diagnose with Alzheimer's Dementia Disease and was also suffering from a heart condition.

The patient was scheduled to arrive on a Monday afternoon. The son had connected with me, as the Hospice Chaplain, and requested that I be present when the patient arrived , to assist with the transfer. Due to the patient's unmanageable behavior, it was anticipated that he would be resistant to the transfer.

The patient was very religious, Catholic charismatic, and was very respectful of religion and religious leaders. Therefore, the son thought that it would be good to have a clergy member present to help soothe the patient's anxiety.

I arrived at the board and care and met with the administrator and staff. It was a health care facility I was familiar with, having previously had other hospice patients as residents. The care givers were good at their work, and the patient's care always appeared to be well managed.

The patient arrived accompanied by his son, a daughter in law, and a long time family friend. I met him at the car and introduced myself. He told me his name was Emilio Cortez. He was unsteady on his feet so I offered my arm as an assist. I walked him into the board and care facility.

The 87 year-old patient appeared younger than his years. He had nearly a full head of white hair, he was slim, and neatly dressed. He appeared to be calm with a pleasant affect.

The staff was able to get him settled in, assigned him a room, and thanked me for my participatory support in helping with the transfer.

He appeared to be pleased with my intervention. I asked if he would like me to pray with Him, and he consented to prayer.

I assured him I would be seeing him on a regular basis, would see him later in the week, and we could read scripture, and pray together each time I visited.

I said a brief prayer with him, and told him *"Good-bye for now,"*

I assured the family, *"I am available at any time,"* said good bye, and left the board and care facility.

The following Thursday I again visited Mr. Cortez. He didn't remember my name, but he remembered I was *"from the church."*

We had an enjoyable visit at which time he told me, *"Religion is very important to me,"* and *"I love to pray."*

I began to realize the extent of his memory impairment when he shared with me some non-essential information.

He said, *"I got laid off, after 35 years."*

I wanted him to be comfortable so I attempted to engage him in conversation.

"I'm sorry to hear that," I said. *"What are you going to do now?"*

"I don't know," he replied, and then continued, *"Elizabeth also lost her job."*

I later learned that Elizabeth had been his wife of 42 years, and had been deceased for 4 years.

Mr. Cortez spoke again,. *'I don't want you tell her (Elizabeth) that I said this, but when she smokes in the house I don't like it.'*

"Have you told her you don't like cigarette smoke?" I asked.

"Oh, no!" he said emphatically, *"that would hurt her feelings!"*

Recognizing that talking was therapy for him, I encourage him *to* talk.

"What else you want to talk about, today?" I asked.

"Not much else," he replied.

During ensuing visits we continued to have conversation which was, at least, meaningful to him.

He talked about being a machinist, and owning his own machine shops, in several different cities. His long term memory appeared to be intact. His short term memory was fleeting. Sometimes good; sometimes, not so good.

As a matter of information, this appears to be a pattern of behavior for Alzheimer / Dementia patients.

Mr. Cortez's condition rapidly declined. During our initial visits he talked about *"Wanting to go home."* He would say, *"This place is nice, but I like my home better."*

As he declined, he became increasingly anxious, and psychotic. His medication had to be increased proportionally. His appetite decreased; he lost 25 pounds in two months.

Eventually, he became bed bound, incontinent of bladder and bowl, and required full assistance with his daily activities.

The board and care staff made him as comfortable as possible. As Chaplain, I increased my frequency of visits to twice a week for on-going spiritual support, and a sense of spiritual connectedness. He always appeared to enjoy prayer, and often held my hand, as I prayed.

Six months after entering the board and care health facility as his residence Mr. Cortez passed away in his sleep, with a peaceful death. I later learned he died clutching a worn crucifix, pressed to his heart.

CHAPTER 36

I Don't Know What's Happening to Me

The door opened, and before I could introduce myself, the tall, red-headed gentleman asked,

"Are you the Chaplain?"

"I am," I replied, "my name is Curtis, *"Are you Mr. Townsend?"*

"Yes. I'm Bill," he said, and held open the door. *"Come on in, Chaplain, I need to talk."*

I walked into the dining room of a neatly kept mobile home. He motioned for me to sit on the sofa across from a rocker-recliner he sat down in.

"Thank you for coming, Chaplain," he began, *"I really do need to talk."*

"It's my pleasure; I'm pleased you asked for me. How can I help?" I asked.

"I'm an agnostic. I've never been active in a church. I'm not even sure there is a God. and, even if there is a God, I don't think he would be interested in me," he said in an honest statement.

"What do you want to do about your belief?" I asked, trying to determine a course of conversation.

"Well, if there is a God, and that's a big if, I don't want to miss out on anything he has to offer," he said.

"How can we approach God with your unbelief?" I asked.

"That's where I was hoping you could help me," he replied.

"I didn't say I don't believe. I said, I'm not sure there is a God," he reiterated.

"This presents a dilemma, Mr. Townsend... Bill. If you are 'not sure there is a God,' how do we go about approaching an unknown God?" I queried.

"Hmmm...., guess you're right, Chaplain. Let's go with the possibility that there is a God out there, and if so, let's ask him to reveal himself to me," he reasoned.

"O.K., I think we can do that. I must caution you, however, be prepared to accept whatever God provides for you," I suggested.

"Fair enough; how do we go about talking to God?" he asked.

"I'm going to talk to him first, just like I'm talking to you. I'm going to pray a prayer and ask him to touch you, in a spiritual way, so as to be able to satisfy you that he is a living, loving, God that does exist," I told him.

"Good. Let's go for it!" he invited.

"Let me pray first, and then, I will let you know when I want you pray the words that I will be praying, which I hope will express the desire of your hear. If they do, then I want you to repeat those words after me," understand I asked him.

He nodded, indicating that he did. With bowed head and closed eyes we were ready to pray. I paused for ten to fifteen seconds gathering my thoughts, after which, I began.

MY PERSONAL PRAYER:

"Heavenly Father, we come to you today on behalf of our new friend Mr. Townsend. You know all about him, and the struggle he is having, in making up his mind about your existence. Guide our words, in a verbal prayer, as we seek your wisdom, to be our wisdom, while we wait upon you for Divine guidance and Providential direction. Let your thinking, be our thinking, and reveal yourself to him. Amen"

I then said to Mr. Townsend, *"I am now going to pray an audible prayer. If the words express the desire of your mind and heart then please repeat them aloud after me. O.K.?"* I asked if he understood.

I then prayed a simple prayer intended to express the desire of Mr. Townsend's heart.

THE PRAYER:

"Eternal God, please give me an open mind, regarding you, and my understanding, in relation to you. Open my eyes that I might know, beyond a reasonable doubt that you do exist, and that you are a caring God, and a God of love. Become real to me and help me to have a spiritual awakening concerning a personal relationship with you. Help me to empty my mind, and set aside my own selfish personal thoughts as to whether or not you do exist. Let me come to know you in a personal way. Thank you for hearing our voices and answering our prayer. Amen"

I opened my eyes to look at Mr. Townsend, who had repeated every word.

Tears were sliding down his cheeks and he began to sob uncontrollably. I placed my hand on his shoulder in an attempt to be comforting and supportive.

He opened his eyes, looked directly into mine and said, *"Chaplain, I don't know what's happening to me, but I feel different. I haven't cried since I was a kid, and here I am crying like a baby."*

He was trembling with emotion. I said to him, *"Relax. Just relax and let go; let go, and let God answer your prayer,"* I said, trying to encourage him.

He said, *"I feel different, like I'm floating on a cloud. I don't understand what is happening. I really do think a Higher Power is trying to tell me something."*

"You have to believe, to receive; believe it, to receive it," I said, again encouraging him to let go, and relax.

"You're right. I'm beginning to get it. How do I say I believe?" he asked.

I suggested to him that he talk to God just like he talked to me. To ask for forgiveness, and, to invite Christ into his heart to become his personal Savior and Lord and Master of his life.

He was silent for a few minutes, and then began to pray on his own:

"God, I really don't know how to pray, but here goes. I really do believe now that there is a Higher Power. If that's you, God, that's O.K. Thank you for helping me to change my mind and believe. I don't know how you did that, but I do know that I have changed my mind. Like I told Chaplain Curtis, I want all you have to offer. I want you to take charge of my life _ of whatever life I have left. The Chaplain has explained to me your Plan of Salvation. How your Son died for all sin, including mine. He told me that by asking for your forgiveness, you would forgive me. I believer that. He also said that the Bible teaches, in order to have eternal life, I needed to invite your Son Christ into my heart. I want to do that now: Lord Jesus, I do want you to come into my heart, save my soul, and give me eternal life. I invite you into my life today."

Amen

He stopped praying. For one, who an hour before had said, *"I'm not even sure there is a God,"* this was a long prayer to a Higher Power _ God, as he *now knew* him.

Mr. Townsend captured all the dynamics of spirituality, in accepting God's love. His eyes were shining again, not with tears this time, but with a new found radiance given only by God.

CHAPTER 37

Everything is Going to be O.K.

The message about a new patient was sketchy but important. The patient was a relative to a member of the executive board of the company where I work. Although we did not, and do not intentionally, show discrimination, in the care and treatment of patients, we certainly did not want to provide any lesser standard of care and treatment for anyone. This was simply *"heads up,"* information.

Subsequently, whether friend, or relative of company executives, everyone was treated equally _ exactly the same _with the best quality of care, and service possible.

Richard Staley met me at the door of his mobile home. I introduced myself as the *"Hospice Chaplain,"* and shook his hand.

"I'm Richard," he said, and invited me inside. We walked through the kitchen into the living room. He motioned for me to sit down on the sofa.

He had introduced himself as *"Richard,"* so I presumed that was what he wanted me to call him. To be sure, I asked, *"Do you prefer to be called by your first or last name?"*

"Richard is fine," he said, *"Just don't call me Dick or Rich,"* he said to me.

"Thank you for requesting to see me, Richard," I answered.

"I really need to talk, Chaplain. I thought you'd be the logical choice, especially, since part of my problem is religious," he said.

"I'm a good listener," I told him, and encouraged him, *"Share with me whatever is on your mind,"* I invited.

"This information is very personal and is going to take a while. How's your time?" he asked.

"Everything we talk about is confidential; clergy parishioner privileged" I assured him.

"My time is your time. Tell me whatever you need to say," I invited.

"Good. That's good. I wouldn't want anyone else knowing my business, Chaplain," he said. *"Where do you want me to start?"* he asked.

"Start anywhere, we work from your agenda" I encouraged him.

He took a deep breath, exhaled. *"As I said, it's a long story."* He stopped talking, pulled out a cigarette from a crumpled pack, lit up, and began.

"Chaplain, I'm a retired Captain of the local fire department. After 20 years in the department I was forced to retire due to a disability; smoke inhalation. I blame myself, in a way, for the damage caused to my lungs. My doctor told me if I gave up smoking the condition of my lungs would improve and become more healthy. "I didn't follow his advice. I kept on smoking these darn cancer sticks. My disability turned into COPD (Chronic Obstructive Pulmonary Disorder), and now I've been diagnosed with lung cancer.

"To top it off, I'm only 63 years-old. My wife Diane is 53 and is still working. We never had any children. We were both orphans. Our parents died when we were kids, and we went from foster home, to foster home. Neither of us was ever adopted.

"Finally, we were old enough to be on our own. I joined the military and Diane became a waitress and started going to night classes at college to pursue her dream of becoming a nurse.

He stopped talking and reached for an oxygen line, attached to a nasal candela. He placed the nosepiece in his nostrils, turned on the oxygen concentrator, and breathed deeply.

"I run out of breathe real fast when I start talking a lot," he explained.

"I don't want to exhaust you, and use up all your energy, or cause respiratory distress.

Would you feel more comfortable to continue your story another time?" I asked.

"No!" he emphatically said." *"I've needed to talk about this for a long time. Just give me a few minutes and I'll continue,"* he told me.

Minutes later he removed the oxygen nose piece and again started talking.

"When I was promoted to Captain by the fire department I was required to take a course on human behavior. I enrolled at the local college in a night class. It was the same college Diane was attending. She was also enrolled in the human behavior class. That's how we met. We went out for coffee a few times, liked each other, and started going together seriously. One thing led to another and we fell in love. I asked her to marry me and she accepted. We've been married ever since; 31 years.

"I'm feeling guilty because I'm going to go away and leave her alone when I die. That's not all that I feel guilty about. I'm also feeling guilty for another reason. Diane has been a faithful wife. I'm afraid I can't say the same. I've been unfaithful several different times, but not in the past ten plus years. I never told her, and she doesn't know. If she did, it would break her heart.

"That's where the religion comes in, Chaplain. I was raised by foster parents. mostly as a Baptist, but I strayed away from the church, and lost a lot of my faith.

"There are some things I need some help with. I need to obtain forgiveness for my adultery and renew my vows of faith..." He stopped talking, and then continued, *"I really need your help with this. I am struggling in knowing whether or not I should confess my sin of adultery to Diane.*

Can you help me, Chaplain?" he asked in a sincere, pleading voice.

"I'll do what I can to help you," I assured him, and continued,

"But in the final analysis, it has to be a personal decision for you to make, as I guide you through the process," I told him

"I'm ready to do anything you suggest, Chaplain. I will trust your judgment," he replied.

"O.K., Richard, let me collect my thoughts," I said. I bowed my head, closed my eyes, and said a silent prayer asking God's intervention and direction in helping Richard to achieve his goals.

Richard patiently waited for my input.

I began by saying, *"Richard, I can't tell you what to do. Neither would I try to tell you what to do, even if I could. Just know, that what I am about to say is what I would do, if I were Baptist, and if I were you."*

"That's good, Chaplain. Give me the idea of what you would do," he invited.

"Richard, the first order of business is to reconcile the alienation from the Lord. If it were me, I would ask God's forgiveness, and ask Christ to re-enter my heart and life, and to take charge, and cleanse me from all unrighteousness. God and Christ tells us in the scriptures that there is no limit to the number of times for forgiveness. So, if I were a Baptist that would be my first step.

Now you say you have not been unfaithful in 'ten plus years.' Is that true, or are you being untruthful with yourself?" I asked for confirmation.
"Yes, Chaplain, that is the truth," he assured me.

"O.K. Richard, again, I can only tell you what I would do, if I were you. Having asked God for forgiveness, you will have received his forgiveness. So the matter rests between God and you.

You say *'more than ten years'* have passed since you was unfaithful and violated your marriage vows, through adultery and infidelity. I believe you, and I can say this. I, personally _ even as a minister _ would not bring up the subject to my wife.

"Why?" You may be asking. Here is the reasoning: If you were sincere when you asked for God's forgiveness for the adultery, God forgave you.

"The reason I would not tell my wife is, because, if I did, it would

help to ease my conscious, and my guilt, but it would transfer the burden of knowledge to my wife. This could very realistically, and easily, destroy her feelings for me and jeopardized her love for me. So, in my opinion, the information about a ten year old adulterous relationship is better off not shared.

"This is especially true now, when love and trust is so much needed in this time of trauma regarding your terminal illness.

"Now Richard, you may not agree with what I would do, and that's O.K., but you asked for my opinion, and I have shared it with you."

"It sounds like it makes sense," he said, agreeing with my reasoning.

"Permit me to share some more thoughts about what I would do, if I were you," I suggested.

"Sure, Chaplain, go ahead," he invited.

"If I were Baptist, and alienated from the church, I would visit churches until I found a church where I could feel comfortable in, and re-connect with that church. For as long as I would be physically able, I would become a faithful attendee and encourage my wife to join me in celebrating my new-found faith. I would even discuss with my wife the possibility of renewing our marriage vows in the church.

"Finally, I would make every effort to make life as meaningful as possible for my wife, and for my marriage. For as long as my health permitted, I would establish a date night where we would go together to the theater, to the movies, or to a restaurant, every week. This would be only a small token of appreciation for the wife beyond the norm.

I conclude by saying, *"I've talked too much, Richard. I imagine you are exhausted.*

"No. Not really, Chaplain. I'm pumped up. I really appreciate your input. I've really needed to talk about all this. Your wisdom and your time is much appreciated," he assured me

"May I pray with you before I leave?" I asked.

"Please do," he invited.

In the ensuing months I was pleased to have a number of follow up visit with Richard. On one of those visit I met his wife Diane. She impressed me as being charming, intelligent, and a supportive spouse.

Through my on-going visits, I learned that Richard had found a Baptist church that both he and Diane enjoyed worshipping with, felt comfortable in, and liked the pastor and his wife.

From the onset of our visits he had appeared to really connect with me, as Chaplain. He subsequently asked me, with his wife Diane present, to baptize him, offer him Holy Communion, and each time we visited, he asked me to bless him and anoint him with oil.

On one of our last visits, before he passed, I noted that, his disease had progressed. He had grown remarkably weaker, and had become bed-bound.

He said to me, *"Chaplain, I am very glad I met you. You have helped me a lot. Even though I know I don't have much longer to live, I know now, with God's help, everything is going to be O.K."*

A week later his prediction came true. With his faithful wife Diane at his bedside, he passed from this life with a peaceful death, into that eternal abode; a place not made with hands called Paradise.

CHAPTER 38

I Ain't (sic) Done Yet...

Virginia Jefferson, a 78 year-old African American female, was a cancer patient who had been given a prognosis of 3 to 6 months to live.

When she initially signed onto the hospice program she had requested to speak to a chaplain. Again, in her own words she had said, *"I want to see a preacher man."*

Her case was assigned to me as her chaplain. I called her home to schedule an appointment for a Spiritual Assessment evaluation for any spiritual needs.

When she answered the phone her voice was strong and clear with a southern accent. I introduced myself and requested an appointment.

"Why do I need you?" she asked.

"I am really calling because you asked for 'a preacher man,' when you entered the hospice program," I answered.

"Yeah, I guess I did; I forgot. When do you want to see me?" she asked.

"At your convenience, Mrs. Jefferson," I told her.

"Well, what about tomorrow?" she said.

"That works for me," I assured her. "Would you want a morning or afternoon appointment?" I asked.

"Afternoon," she replied, and continued, *"I usually sleep in until about 9:30 or 10:00."*

"Good. It's an appointment then, I'll see you between 1 and 2 PM. Is that O.K.?" I asked"

"Yes. That will be O.K.," she said, agreeing with the time.

I arrived at the home at 1:30, knocked on the door and waited. The door soon opened and I observed a tall, thin, dark-haired woman. Before I could speak she asked, *"Are you the Chaplain?*

"I am. My name is Curtis," I said.

"I'm Virginia," she answered, and shook my hand.

We entered the living room. She motioned toward the couch and said, *"Sit down and take a load off your feet."* I recognized a southern accent expression.

"What part of the south are you from?" I asked.

"How do you know I'm from the south? Who told you I was from the south?" she asked.

"Your southern accent gave you away," I told her smiling.

"Yeah, I guess I do have a southern drawl," she replied.

"Your accent is charming and your voice is pleasant," I told her.

"Thank you, Chaplain. That's nice of you to say," she replied.

She appeared to be one of a kind. She told me she had grown up in Alabama and, in her own words, was *"the target of more racial discrimination and prejudice than you could shake a stick at,"* using another southern expression in a thick, southern accent.

For the past 20 years she had lived in southern California. At the time of my contact she resided in a luxury apartment complex, in an up-scale neighborhood.

Mrs. Jefferson was easy to talk to, and was kind in her demeanor. She enjoyed talking, even though she had to stop often to catch her breath. She had been diagnosed with emphysema years before from heavy smoking. The emphysema had exacerbated, and more recently she had been diagnosed with end stage Chronic Obstructive Pulmonary Disorder (COPD), a terminal illness. She also had an accompanying diagnosis called Congestive Heart Failure (CHF). She was fiercely independent, lived alone, and said, *"I want to keep it that way.*

We talked about anything, and everything; politics, local news, her illness, and her family. She was quick to tell me about her family. *"I have a son and daughter who still live in the south. They want me to come and live with one of them, but that's not going to happen. I ain't (sic) done yet,"* she said with emphasis.

She continued, *"I'll live alone for as long as I live."*

"What happens when you are no longer able to live by yourself?" I asked.

"I will live alone for as long as I live, then I'll die," she boldly replied.

The subject finally turned to religion. *"What is you religious preference, "*I asked.

"I've been a Baptist all my life," she replied.

"Are you connected to a church in the area?" I inquired.

"No. I've been several times, but I have never joined one," she answered, and then went on to say, *"I've sort of turned off on the church. Not on God mind you, but on the church."*

"Want to talk about it?" I invited.

"No"… she started to say more, and then added, *"Yes, I need to get this out of my craw,"* another southern expression. She continued, *"The pastor of my church back home was a real scoundrel. He had been pastor there for fifteen years, was married with two teenage children. He took up with, and ran away with, a young divorcee who had joined the church. He abandoned his family and the church. So, I'm a little sour on churches, right now,"* she said, and stopped talking.

I was silent for several minutes and then said, *"I can understand you frustration and disappointment, Mrs. Jefferson. But I need to say, as angry as you are, it's unfair to compare all churches to the actions of one pastor. Don't you think that's unfair?"* I asked for her opinion

"Well, I didn't really mean to blame the church _ since the people are the church _ but usually, when you think of a pastor, you think about using the word church," she said, explaining her reasoning.

"Would you want me to facilitate a Baptist minister to come see you, and pray with you?" I asked.

"No. I was told that you are a minister. Is that right?" she demanded.

"Yes, I am. I am a non-denominational minister," I replied.

"You sound like my kind of person; I like you, so you can come pray with me," she invited.

"Good. I will be pleased to have you think of me as your pastor. I will consider it a pleasure to come and pray with you." I told her.

"Good. Let's do that right now," she said.

"What would you want me to pray for?" I asked.

"Pray God will take me home, before I get so bad that I can't live by myself," she requested, smiling.

I will pray asking God to grant unto you the desires of your heart, Mrs. Jefferson. Will that do?" I asked her.

"Couldn't have said it better pastor. I'm liking (sic) you more all the time," she said.

"Thank you. I like you, Mrs. Jefferson. You are a delightful lady," I again complimented her. I read some scripture from the Psalms, said some prayers, blessed her and anointed her with oil.

She thanked me, told me to *"come back real soon,"* shook my hand and said *"good-bye."*

Over the next several months I visited Mrs. Jefferson a number of times. She encouraged me to read scripture to her, pray with her, and invited me back time, and time again.

On one of our last visits, I had called ahead, made an appointment, and was expecting to find her home, as per usual. I arrived, and knocked on her door several times, but did not receive an answer.

As I turned to leave, I observed a lady wearing a straw hat pulled down over her face. She was wearing a red and white checkered bandana around her neck.

She was pushing a two-wheeled grocery cart, with several grocery items such as bananas, bread and milk in the cart. As she approached I asked, *"Have you seen Mrs. Jefferson?"*

She stopped, pulled off her hat and said, *"I'm Mrs. Jefferson."* She burst into laughter at my surprised look.

Both of Mrs. Jefferson's grown children came to see visit with her before she passed. I had the .privilege of meeting them, and assured them Mrs. Jefferson was receiving the best care and treatment possible, through the hospice program, and that she was doing O.K., and coping beautifully.

They thanked me profusely for reporting to them and said that they could see *"Mother is getting good care."*

The last time I attempted to contact Mrs. Jefferson by telephone, I did not receive an immediate answer. I was not overly concerned. I remembered another time, when I had arrived to see her, she had not been home, and had been shopping at the grocery store, just one block from her apartment.

I continued to try and connect with her by phone. I called multiple times and never received an answer. I became concerned and called the R.N. Case Manager, who said she was scheduled to see Mrs. Jefferson later that morning.

At 11 A.M. I received notification from the case manager that she had arrived at the apartment, knocked on the door, and never received an answer.

She told me she contacted the manager, who had a master key to the apartment. They entered the apartment to find that Mrs. Jefferson had passed away, sitting in her overstuffed *"easy chair,"* (as she called it). She had been watching television; the TV set was still on.

The coroner determined she had sustained a *"massive heart attack"* which, according to the coroner, would have resulted in *"sudden death."* It was comforting to learn that, in dying, she had not suffered.

CHAPTER 39

Why Shouldn't I be Mad?

I was informed by the social worker that the new hospice patient wanted to see a Chaplain. I was assigned to her case.

I called her home, spoke with the twenty-four hour care giver, Pauline, and scheduled an appointment for a spiritual assessment to evaluate and determine her spiritual needs.

From her medical records I learned that the patient was a cancer survivor. Fifteen years earlier she had been diagnosed with breast cancer, had a radial mastectomy, underwent chemotherapy and radiation therapy, and went into remission.

Now, the cancer had returned. The undetected cancer, resulting in her most recent diagnosis, had metastasized (spread) to other organs and was declared *"inoperable."*

As a result, she had been re-diagnosed with a terminal illness, and a probable prognosis between 3 to 6 months. Her doctor had referred her to a hospice program.

Elizabeth White, a 51 year-old Caucasian female had beaten the odds. For the past fifteen years she had been cancer free, and had lived a reasonably normal life with cancer; now, she was dying with it.

Betty, (as she liked to be called), was angry. She said, *"I thought I had outlived cancer, but now, I have it again."*

Her anger had turned *outside.* She was angry at her oncologist, for not detecting the reoccurring cancer sooner. She was angry at her neighbors for their barking dogs, she was angry at the world in general, and she was especially angry at God. She was more than angry; she was just plain mad.

At the time of my first visit, she was experiencing a rapidly declining physical deterioration.

She was no longer able to drive. Her strength had decreased to the point where, she could no longer trust herself to be safe behind the wheel. Therefore, she lost her ability on her own to move about for any distance, thus, losing a major part of her independence.

She was mad about this, which she had every right to be. Independence, and maintaining independence is a very important part of anyone's life, even when one is well and healthy.

Obviously, anger is O.K.; the Bible says, *"Be angry and sin not," Ephesians 4:26.* Of course, sin comes when one's anger goes out of control and one lashes out at others in rude and disrespectful ways.

As indicated, Betty's anger had become an obsession with her. A type of madness, and had been turned *outside* and verbally expressive. Subsequently, she was very difficult to work with.

Nevertheless, the chaplain's responsibility is _ as is every member of the hospice team _ to work from the patient's agenda and that, we did.

I remember our first meeting:

I had met the 24 hour, live-in, care giver _ the third one in as many weeks, I was told; she had hired and fired two others _ who showed me into the living room, where I met Betty at her hospital bed side. I introduced myself.

"My name is Curtis. I'm the hospice Chaplain who has been assigned to you, Mrs. White." I said.

She accepted my extended hand with a firm grip and said, *"I looked forward to meeting you, Chaplain.*

"I wanted to meet you," I replied, *"to let me know who you are, and to let you know, who I am."* We joined in laughter.

To establish rapport we each made small talk, and then she said, *"Let's talk about what I wanted to see you for."*

"O.K.," I agreed, *"How can I help?"*

"I'm not really sure. I needed to ask you about a few things; to get a second opinion on some things that have been bothering me. I don't know where to start," She said.

"Start anywhere," I encouraged her.

"My daughter wants me to sell my home I've had for 35 years and to move in with them. I don't want to do that, but she and her husband keep insisting," she said, and continued, *"What do you think I should do?"*

"I'm not in a position to give you advice, Betty. But you appear to still be in control of your independence, so it sounds like it would be your choice," I answered.

"I think so," she said, *"I'll just let them know I'm not going to sell my home."*

"The other things I struggle with, and want to talk to you about, happened sixteen years ago. I let my grandson Mark, who had just gotten his drivers' License, borrow my new car. He was driving on the freeway, got hit and killed by a drunk driver. I have had this on my conscious, and mind, and have blamed myself all these years," she said.

And continued, *"My other grandson, Mike, his twin brother, went into shock over the death of his brother. He started using prescription drugs for depression, and eventually overdosed on prescription drugs. The coroner declared his death as, an accidental overdose. But I think he took his own life. I also blame myself for his death."*

"It sounds like you've had a lot of losses," I empathized.

"Yes, Chaplain, and now, I'm losing my own life. It's not fair. Is there any good reason I shouldn't be mad?" she asked, making a statement question.

She had a valid point, from her own perspective. I learned that she felt God had turned his back on her.

"I've never been a very religious person, and I didn't raise my family to be, either. I think God may be getting even with me, and punishing me," she concluded..

I was silent for a few minutes, allowing her to reflect on her own words; what she had just said. Then, I spoke. *"Betty, I don't think God works like that. While God is in control of the universe, he doesn't cause bad things to happen to good people. The activity of life experiences, of human life, often encounters adverse circumstances and situations. Permit me to give you an example.*

"When your grandson Mark was hit and killed by a drunk driver, God did not cause that to happen. It happened because a man made a decision to drink alcohol, and drive under the influence of that alcohol.

"As for your other grandson Mike, he was severely affected by the death of his twin brother. That is an understandable reaction to a tragic event. While the tragedy itself pushed him to the edge, he had to make a decision to turn to prescription drugs as a means of relief, to deal with it.

"As hard as this might sound, Betty, the decision, and risk of losing his life through the use of those dangerous, habit-forming drugs, was carefully explained to him by his doctor, and was well known to him. While you think he committed suicide, by taking an overdose, I don't agree. I think he received some relief from his depression, and grief, through the use of the medications, and that he became addicted, and more, and more dependent upon them.

"I think his reasoning was, 'if I receive a little benefit from taking a few, I will receive much more benefit from taking lot.' *"Subsequently, he became so dependent upon them, until it pushed him over the edge, and he overdosed. That is my opinion, Betty,"* I said to her.

I paused for effect and, to let her absorb, and process what information I had provided, and then, I made a most important statement.

"Betty, I want you to listen carefully to what I am going to say. It is a normal reaction to place blame, and perhaps normal for you, to

want to accept blame, for the tragic deaths of your grandsons. But just know, it was not God's fault, and it was not your fault.

"The grandson Mark, who was killed in the auto accident, was just that. An accident caused by a drunk driver, who made a terrible choice and decision, to drink and drive while under the influence of alcohol.

"As far as your other grandson Mike's tragic death is concerned, it was a permanent solution, to a temporary problem. The temporary problem was his deep, profound bereavement, grief and sadness over the loss of his brother. A problem which could have, and should have, been addressed through clinical, psychotherapy counseling, and, a bereavement support group; not to obtain relief only through prescription drugs.

"Betty, in either case, neither death was your fault. Therefore, you should not blame yourself. I know what you're thinking, that is, 'It is easy for me to say, but, it is very difficult for you to accept.'

"I agree with you. But when you accept blame, for something that is not your fault, and you keep blaming yourself, you need to come to a decision to forgive yourself. ?" I concluded with a very important question. *Have you done that, Betty?"*

I again stopped to let her reflect, on the information I had provided, and the question. She was silent for a time and then answered.

"No, I never did. I didn't even think about that. I never looked at it like that, before," she confessed.

"Does that sound like something you would like to do?" I asked.

Before she could answer, I made another important comment.

"Betty, you asked for help, and my opinion. Please know, I am not trying to tell you what to do, or how to do it. I am only suggesting some alternative views to consider," I assured her.

"How do I forgive myself?" she asked.

"It's really quite simple. Just talk to yourself in the third person. For instance I will give you an example:"

TALKING IN THIRD PERSON:

"Betty, I know you have been blaming yourself for the death of your grandsons Mark and Mike. I want you to know, it was not, and is not, your fault, that either of them died. It was a life happening tragedy, in the human experience.

"So, what I want you to do, right now, and say in, talking to yourself:

'Even though, I Betty, have accepted guilt and responsibility, for the death of my grandsons, I was not at fault; I forgive myself, for any blame I have accepted. I do forgive myself, and let go of the blame; I will walk through the pool of pain to the other side. I love myself, and will help myself to heal."

She remained silent again for a time, and I could see tears forming. This was a *good* sign. She was getting in touch with her feelings. I encouraged her to express her emotions.

"Betty, don't try and hold anything back. Let it all out. Let the tears flow and empty your mind," I encouraged her. She silently wept.

A knock sounded at the door, and the care giver answered. Betty's daughter Jennifer arrived.

I introduced myself, *"Hi, I'm Chaplain Curtis. Your mother and I have been enjoying a visit,"* I told her.

"I'm pleased to meet you, Chaplain. I'm Jennifer. Thank you for visiting my mother. I've heard good things about you." she said, complimenting me.

"You are too kind," I told her, returning the compliment

I decided it was time to leave mother and daughter alone to visit.

I told Betty *"I will be in touch."* I said to Jennifer, *"It's been nice meeting you,"* "and to all, *"good bye, for now."* The caregiver Pauline, had re-appeared; she motioned for me to follow her to the door for her to see me out.

In subsequent visit I observed Betty's demeanor soften toward the care giver and myself.

She remained very adamant about what she did, and did not want, as far as her care was concerned.

She tenaciously clung to her independence.

She never stopped talking about her grandsons. She told me she had brought herself to a level of absolution concerning her guilt, and no longer fully blamed herself. She hastened to say that, *"After all these years, I struggle to accept Mark and Mike's death. It continues to seem surreal."* I was able to give her some suggestions for closure which appeared to help.

Betty's disease progressed, and she became increasingly weak, with decreased energy. her appetite disappeared, and she lost approximately 25 pounds in two months. She became bed bound and needed assistance with all her daily activities.

We talked about God and her relationship *to* God. She told me that, *"I made my peace with God."* Her actions and demeanor attested to a visible change. She appeared to become more compassionate with those who cared for her.

Despite the apparent change, at last count (according to her), she had hired and fired 17 different live-in caregivers.

On a Monday afternoon, the week before her death, she requested a joint meeting with her daughter, son-in-law, and the hospice clinical staff team, including myself. She took the opportunity to address them. Although she was weak in body, her voice was strong.

"I want to say. I'm not mad anymore. I also want to thank everyone for the good care you have given me. All have been wonderful. I need to apologize for any mean words I have used, or any action I have taken to offend anyone. Please forgive me," she said, and a tear streaked down her cheek. That was her message.

The following Sunday morning, at 3:10 A.M., caregiver Pauline discovered Betty had quit breathing; she passed in her sleep, free from pain and comfortable, with a peaceful mind.

CHAPTER 40

One Day I'll Take Care of it...

William Nelson had shared with me, as a Hospice Chaplain that he had lived with his handicap for twenty-five years. The career connected handicap was tragic. He had been a railroad brakeman with a major train company. At age 25, on one icy December morning, he had slipped while performing his job and fell underneath a box car. He lost both legs just above the knees.

As a result of the accident _ Billy, as he liked to be called _ had, at first partially accepted his handicap. He went through therapy, rehabilitation, and was in time fitted for prostheses.' He related that he never fully *"learned to use the artificial legs."* He said, he *"always felt uncomfortable, and was afraid of falling."* Subsequently, he was self-confined to a wheel chair, which he had learned to use very well.

He received a moderate settlement from the Rail Road Company, and early medical retirement, with medical and hospital benefit coverage for the rest of his life.

Billy and his family moved from the mid-west to California, where he bought a piece of property and had a custom home built, to accommodate his handicap movement in the wheel chair. All doorways were 4 feet wide, the hallways were 5 feet wide, and the three bath rooms were designed to accommodate his personal needs.

He and wife Hazel had two sons and a daughter. The kids still lived at home and had full- time jobs. Although she didn't need to, Hazel also worked. They managed comfortably on his retirement income, and had learned to live a reasonably normal life.

To help him cope with his handicap, Billy had turned to alcohol.

He also told me that he was *"a heavy smoker."* At the age of 50 he had acute emphysema, and was compelled to constantly use oxygen.

He continued to smoke, even with the oxygen turned on. Smoking and oxygen don't mix.

There is always a grave danger of explosion and fire. That is exactly what happened to Billy.

One morning after the wife and kids had left for work, he was sitting on the patio in his wheel chair using his portable oxygen tank, smoking. There was an explosion which started a minor fire. Billy sustained major burns on his face and neck, but was able to put out the fire.

He was alert enough to call 911. The paramedics came and took him to the ER of a local hospital where he was treated for his burns. The hospital notified the hospice agency, who was able to address his wound care after his discharge from the hospital back to his home.

Billy said, initially, when he started hospice care, *"since I am not very religious,"* he refused the spiritual support. *"I did not want spiritual care from the Chaplain."* After his most recent accident with the fire he had changed his mind and requested *"to talk with a Chaplain."*

I was notified, called his home, and scheduled an appointment for that afternoon. His daughter Sarah was present when I arrived to keep the appointment. She answered the door.

"Come in, Chaplain," she said, after I introduced myself. *"We've been expecting you. Daddy's in his bed room,"* she continued, and led me down the hallway to his room.

Billy sat upright in his hospital bed, smoking a cigarette and reading a National Rifle Association magazine.

I introduced myself. *"Good afternoon, Mr. Nelson,"* I said, extending my hand in greeting. He accepted my hand and squeezed it in a firm grip.

"Call me Billy; that's my name," he invited.

"O.K.," I replied, *"My name is Chaplain Curtis."*

"Have a seat, Chaplain Curtis," he said.

"I see you are reading an NRA magazine. Are you a member," I asked.

"Oh, yes, been a member for years. Before my accident I was a devoted hunter. I love guns and have owned them, and fired them, all my life. Even after my accident, I would go to the firing range," he answered. *"I used to collect guns,"* he said, and pointed to a gun cabinet standing in the corner of his bed room.

I looked at the glass-enclosed gun cabinet and noticed it contained a number of pistols and rifles.

"I also sleep with one," he said, raising his pillow revealing what appeared to be a 45 caliber handgun.

"Are you able to handle all this O.K., surrounded by your oxygen tube, and overhead lift, plus all your medications." I asked.

"Oh, sure," no problem; piece of cake,"* he replied, smiling.

"You asked to see me, Billy. How can I help?" I asked.

"I've never been a religious man..." he began, stopped talking, and then continued, *"But, if there is a God, I'm mad at him."*

"Want to talk about it?" I asked

"Yes. Yes, I do," he answered and continued, *"Why would a so-called loving God let me lose my legs, and then at age 50 _ soon to be 51 _ let me get cancer?"*

His recent lung cancer diagnosis had devastated him. The doctor had told him *"There is nothing more we can do for you,"* and had referred him to the hospice agency, where I serve as a Chaplain.

"Billy, I don't believe God 'let you lose your legs' or caused you 'get lung cancer,'" I told him.

"You think it was my own fault, Chaplain?" he asked.

"No. I don't think the accident was your fault. I think accidents

happen due to circumstances. Sometimes they are caused. But it sounds like yours was a freak accident; no one's to blame, and no one is to blame. As far as the lung cancer is concerned, you could be at least, partly responsible for that. By your own admission, you are now, and have been all your life a heavy smoker. Medical research and science has proven that smoking can cause lung cancer." I stopped talking to let him absorb and process the information I had provided.

He was silent for a few minutes and then spoke. *"I guess I've never looked at it like that before,"* he said.

"It's worth considering," I told him.

"Yeah, I guess so," he agreed.

"Billy, do you have a religious preference?" I asked.

"Can't say that I have," he replied, and continued, *"I've only been inside a church for funerals and weddings,"*

"Do you have a belief system?" I asked, trying to find common ground on which to communicate with him.

"Well, I used to believe in a Higher Power. Now, I'm not so sure," he honestly answered.

"Billy, you requested to see a Chaplain. I am a Chaplain; how can I help you?" I asked again.

"I don't know," he replied. He was brutally honest.

He continued to talk, *"I'd like to believe, but I can't get past blaming God _ or a Higher Power _ for my accident. And now, my cancer, I heard you when you said it was no body's fault, just an accident, but I'm not sure I'm buying that."*

"I do take responsibility for my cancer, though. It does make sense that smoking does cause lung cancer." he concluded his statement, and made a facial grimace.

I immediately recognized the sign and symptom of pain. I asked him, *"Billy, are you in pain?"*

"Yeah, I gotta (sic) take some more of that darn morphine. I only take it when my pain gets so bad I can't stand it. It takes care of the pain, but dopes me up so that I want to sleep all the time. I

don't like that. I want to be as alert as possible. I really hate to take the morphine, but it does help ease my pain. One of these days I will take care of it in another way," he said with a wink, and patted his pillow.

I remembered the 45 caliber handgun I had seen only minutes before when he had raised the pillow.

"Does that mean you would take your own life?" I asked

"Naw, I was just blowin' off steam," he responded.

He took a medication treatment and in less than twenty minutes he began to nod off.

Sensing he was going to slide into sleep I began preparing to leave.

"Would you want me to pray with you before I leave, Billy?" I asked.

"I think I'll pass, Chaplain," he replied, and then said, *"Maybe next time."*

"Does that mean you want to see me again?" I asked.

"Yes," he said, *"I'd like that,"* I shook his hand and said, *"Good bye for now,"* and let myself out.

My visit with Billy Nelson revealed a potentially serious problem. Without meaning to, he had made a bold statement. He had inadvertently expressed suicidal ideations. The possibility of him taking his own life was a reality.

I reported the incident to the hospice executive staff, and to the assigned hospice care team.

Working with the family, the means, method, and opportunity for him taking his own life were eliminated. The guns were removed from the home and taken to his best friend's home. A thorough search was made by the family of the house to make sure there were no weapons available to Billy.

I suspected he would be angry with me for alerting the family to his possible suicide intentions. Surprisingly, he did not object to the removal of the guns, and neither did he mention it, and he did not appear to be angry with me. In fact, to the contrary, on subsequent visits he appeared more cheerful and appeared to gain more respect for me, and to let me pray with him.

He told me that he was *"Thinking about getting back his faith."* At the same time, he said his pain level was *"increasing daily, and that he was finding it more, and more difficult to not take the morphine."* More than once he said, *"I just wish I could die; this is no kind of life."*

Billy asked for, and I provided, some spiritual reading material. He thanked me and said, *"It helped."*

From a spiritual perspective, I thought he was making progress. I asked him, *"Would you like a Bible?"* He refused saying, *"No. Not now,"*

Over the next several weeks his condition deteriorated and he declined remarkably. He became incontinent of bowel and bladder, and was no longer able to transfer, from his bed to the wheel chair, thus, became bed bound.

On a Thursday afternoon he had his daughter call my office and request another visit.

"Daddy said he wants to see you, and talk to you, Chaplain, He said it is important," she said.

"Does he want to see me right away?' I asked, and then I told her to tell him, *"I could come today, if he wants me to."*

"Let me ask him," she replied. I told her to take her time, and the phone went silent. Several minutes passed as I waited for the answer. Then I heard her voice again.

"Chaplain, Daddy said 'Not today; tomorrow in the morning,'" she said.

I scheduled the appointment for the next day, Friday before noon, *"Tell him I look forward to seeing him,"* I told her. She said, *"I will."*

At 3:30 A.M. Friday morning, I received a call from the on-call nurse that the family was requesting my presence. I responded to the call and drove to the home. Multiple emergency vehicles were parked around the house when I arrived. I sensed a tragedy. I was met by a police officer who informed me that Johnny had committed suicide. He had shot himself in the head with a handgun no one knew he had, that had been hidden under his mattress.

What was so *"important,"* that Billy wanted to talk to me about? Did his increased pain drive him over the edge? Could I have talked him out of taking his own life? Prevented his suicide if I had of been able to see him earlier?

So many questions; God only knows the answer.

CHAPTER 41

I Wish I Could Die!

The patient introduced himself to me at the front door. *"I'm Paul Collins, Chaplain,"* he said, *"Thanks for coming."*

"My name is Chaplain Curtis, Mr. Collins. It's my pleasure to visit with you," I replied.

"You know, Chaplain... or Pastor... what should I call you? Pastor or Chaplain?" he asked.

"Call me either one. The terms are actually synonymous," I told him.

"O.K., I'll call you Chaplain. You call me Paul," he said, and continued, *"As I was saying, I've never been sick a day in my life, have never had surgery, or a broken bone, and haven't been to a doctor in twenty years. Now, I have everything in the world wrong with me,"* he said.

Paul Collins had recently been diagnosed with a dual diagnosis, i.e., insulin dependent diabetes and full blown AIDS (Acquired Immune Deficiency)

Paul went on to say, *"I'm 43 years old, Chaplain. I'm too young to die, but the doctor said I was going to,"* he confirmed the terminal diagnosis.

"Paul, we are all going to die; some just get there sooner" I empathized.

"Yes. I of course know that's true, but you usually don't die before your parents," he replied.

"That's a valid point," I agreed, and then asked, *"Do your parents live locally?"*

He told me, *"No. They live in Hawaii. I was just getting ready to visit them when I collapsed at work and was taken to the ER."*

Paul said he was a professional hair stylist. By his own admission, he confessed he was Gay and, that he had contracted AIDS.

He shared his story: *"When I was 13 years old I knew I was different. All my buddies were starting to look at, and talk about girls. I didn't have that interest. I was more interested in being with the guys. As I moved into my late teens I became more interested and began to experiment with sex. Once I started, I couldn't stop. Sex became an obsession with me. I couldn't get enough. I was a regular at gay bars, and went home with a different guy every night.* He stopped talking, as though he was trying to remember every detail, and then continued.

"Then I met this guy who I really fell for. He was a body builder; tall, blonde, good looking, and in my eyes beautiful. I fell in love with him, and he said he loved me. We moved in together.

"Even though we were lovers, I found out later that, he was very much in demand, fickle, and promiscuous. This I didn't learn until we had been together for two years. I came home unexpectedly one day and found him with another guy. We had a big fight and I moved out. I was very hurt; I felt betrayed.

"Up until this time I had been very discreet about my being gay. I hadn't even told my parents. I am an only child. I was afraid that they would disown me. But after my break-up with Tom I didn't care anymore. At age 38 I came out of the closet.

"I told my parents. They were surprised, but assured me that, 'we are your parents, and you are our son; we love you.' The bottom line was, they said, 'It has to be your choice, son.'

"To make a long story shorter, I then threw caution to the winds

and had multiple sex partners with unprotected, and unsafe sex. I knew I should have been more careful, but I wasn't."

He again stopped talking for a few minutes and then continued.

"I suspected I had AID for some time. I've noticed changes in my body, decreased energy, decreased strength and fatigue at the end of the day."

"I was hoping I was wrong. I know AIDS is fatal. I wasn't going to tell anyone, and then I collapsed at the salon."

He stopped talking again, looked me in the eye, and said. *"Now, you know my life story, Chaplain. What can I do?"* he invited my opinion.

"What do you want to do, Paul?" I asked.

"I'm not sure. I wish I could contact everyone I've had sex with and let them know they are at risk," he thoughtfully said, and then asked, *"Do you think that is a possibility, Chaplain?"*

"Paul, there is a confidentiality issue with what I am going to mention to you, and you may not be comfortable with it. And that's O.K." I told him, and continued, *"Paul, I don't think it would not be possible to contact all your partners. But perhaps there is a way to get the information out to some. Do you have a close or best friend?"* I asked.

"Yes. Why do you ask?" he wanted to know.

"If you feel comfortable with what I am going to mention to you, perhaps you could ask your friend to share information at the gay bars you have visited. At least, this would get the information out to those whom you have partnered with, that they are at risk," I said.

"I wouldn't have a problem with that, Chaplain," he said. *"That's a good idea. I'll call my best friend Carl and see if he would be comfortable in sharing this information with others."*

"Paul, I have to be very frank and honest with you. As a hospice professional, and Chaplain, I am not suggesting that this is the course of action you should take; just know that. I am simply trying to explore alternative measures available to you," I assured.

I wanted Paul to specifically know, and understand, that I was not trying to tell him what to do. And further, that the decision for any action, on his part, would have to be his choice.

We spent another half hour talking and Paul told me what he really wanted to do for his 44th birthday _ which was one month away _ was to go to Hawaii to see his parents, and to reconcile with his grandparents, who also lived in Hawaii, and who, six year before, when he came out of the closet, had told him, they *'Never wanted to see him again, and didn't want anything to do with him.'*

His problem: He didn't have any money; he hadn't worked in over six months and was barely making ends meet. I filed this away in my memory and secretly vowed to help him make his dream come true.

I sensed that Paul was exhausted from all the conversation which appeared to have sapped his energy. And I told him, *"I don't want to wear you out, so I'll bring my visit to a close.*

May I pray with you before I leave? I asked.

Oh, yes, please do, Chaplain. You have really set my mind at ease today. I can't thank you enough," he replied.

"Just knowing you have been helped is thanks enough, Paul," I again reassured him.

I said some prayers, gave him a blessing and anointed him with oil.

"I will see you, when I see you," I told him. He shook my hand, smiled, and said, *"Ditto."*

I wanted to help him with his 44th birthday celebration in Hawaii, if he had the strength and energy to make the trip, I thought something could be done to assist him.

I contacted a non-profit "Wish" Foundation and asked for their help. They assured me they would *"try to make the trip for Paul possible."*

A week went by and it was getting time for my weekly visit with Paul. I had been hoping to have some good news for him from the non-profit "Wish" organization, but I had not heard from them.

Early afternoon I did receive a call from them. The "Wish" Foundation was granting the request I had facilitated. They would pay all his expenses and wanted to know when he wanted them to schedule flying and lodging accommodations. I told them I was going to see Paul later that day and that I would find out, and let them know.

I called Paul's home. A 24 hour care-giver who had been placed, and was being paid for, by his family answered the phone. I told her who I was and asked her to tell Paul I would see him late that afternoon.

I arrived to find Paul up in the kitchen eating a snack. He shook my hand and said, *"It's good to see you, Chaplain."*

I learned that he was having a burst of energy and felt better, and stronger, than he had for some time. I was glad that he was feeling better.

I said, *"I have some good news for you, that will make you feel even better, Paul."*

"Oh, yeah, what's the news?" he asked.

"You're going to Hawaii to celebrate your birthday with your parents," I told him.

"How...? What...? When am I going?" he stammered.

"Slow down! Relax! Let me tell you about it," I said.

I shared with him how the "Dream" Foundation was sponsoring his trip and covering all the expenses.

He was excited, *"I can't believe it; I just can't believe it, Chaplain,"* he repeated.

"Believe it, Paul. It's true. You are going to Hawaii," I assured him. *"Now we have to set an agenda for you, so the flight and hotel accommodations can be made,"* I told him.

Together we worked out a realistic agenda and I called the "Wish" Foundation who made the accommodations.

Arrangements were made with a sister hospice organization in Hawaii to follow Paul's care during his time in Hawaii. Plans were made with the airline to accommodate his wheel chair and oxygen on his flights. According to the airline Paul would receive VIP treatment for both departing and return flights.

Paul was elated; he could not have been happier. A 43 _ almost 44 _ year old man acting like a kid.

When Paul returned from Hawaii he called my office and requested a visit. I call his home and confirmed that he was rested up enough for a visit. His care giver assured me that he was.

I drove to his home. The care giver let me in and led me to his bedroom. Paul flashed me a and said *"I've got lots to tell you Chaplain." "I had a wonderful time with my parents."*

He continued, *"My grandparents 'forgave me,'* (his words), *for my 'wayward behavior,'* (their words). He continued, *"Chaplain, I am tired from the trip and the activities, and I am tired of this illness. I wish I could die,"* he emphatically said.

I noted that he was struggling to stay awake. His strength and energy were failing. The added physical stress of the trip and activities, and the emotional strain, had taken a toll on his already compromised physical condition.

Paul nodded off, and then awakened with a start. He opened his eyes and said, *"Chaplain, I really want to thank you for all that you have done, and especially for the trip. I can now die in peace knowing my grandparents are no longer mad at me."*

"You are very welcome, Paul. I will write a letter to the "Wish" Foundation thanking them, for you," I told him.

Recognizing that sleep and rest were more important to him than a continuing visit, I told him, *"I'm going to leave now, Paul, you need your rest."*

He nodded in agreement, and mouthed the words, *"Thank you."*

I said a brief prayer with him, shook his Hand, and walked out of the room.

The following day I was notified that Paul had slipped into a comma and had never awakened.

Paul died at 4:45 A.M., Four days after returning from Hawaii where, with his family he had celebrated his 44th birthday. Paul passed from this to another life

When he said, *"I wish I could die,"* God was listening; his wish was granted.

CHAPTER 42

Why Did God Let This Happen?

Robert Lyman and his Wife Mary, lived in a two bed room apartment in a small suburb of Los Angeles, California, where they had lived since their marriage ten years before. Robert was 35 and Mary was 32 years old. They had two children, a boy and a girl, Calvin and Carrie. Calvin was 8 and Carrie 6.

The Lyman's were a deeply religious family. Robert was a truck driver, and Mary a stay-at-home mom; a wife, mother and homemaker. For all intent and purpose an ideal family; the perfect family That perfection had been marred; Robert had recently been diagnosed with a kidney disease, called renal failure, and was not a candidate for dialysis. The diagnosis was terminal with no chance for recovery.

Robert was referred by his doctor to the hospice program where I serve as chaplain. When I met them they were still trying to process the devastating news. They had not yet told the children about their father's illness.

I was in their home by appointment arranged while the children were in school. I introduced myself to Robert and his wife.

"My name is Curtis. I am the hospice chaplain," I said.

He extended his hand in greeting and said, *"Welcome Chaplain, we are glad you came to visit. Our pastor was here yesterday."*

I sat down on the edge of Robert's bed, where he had invited me to sit. Wife Mary sat on a straight back chair at the foot of the bed. Her eyes brimmed with tears as she looked at her husband.

"What is your denomination?" I asked.

"We are Christian; we attend a Pentecostal church," he replied.

"It's good to hear the church and pastor are supportive," I said.

"Oh yes, they are very supportive," he replied, and continued, *"we have had many phone calls and some visit by the members. The pastor is in touch with a visit or a call every day."*

To gain rapport, and work from his agenda, and at the same time be supportive, I asked a question to which I already knew the answer.

"What did your doctor tell you about your illness?" I asked.

"He said that I have 'renal failure, and that there is nothing more that they can do for me because I am not a dialysis candidate,'" he answered

"What does that mean to you?" I asked, trying to establish a course of discussion intervention.

"It means they can't do anything more for me, and that I am going to die," he replied and teared up.

"How can I help, Mr. Lyman?" I asked.

He wiped away tears, gained his composure and said, *"Call me Robert, Chaplain,"* and finally spoke, *"Well, you can pray for me and my family."*

"I will be pleased to do that. Is there anything else you need to talk about?" I encouraged him to open up.

"Yes. Yes there is, Chaplain. Can you tell me why God would let this happen to me? I am a devout believer, take my family to church regularly, I support the church with my money, and I am a good provider, and not a bad person. I try to follow the Golden Rule (do unto others as you would have others do unto you). *I don't understand why God would cause, or let, me get a terminal illness at 35 years of age, especially since I have small children"* he ended his questioning. Tears ran down his cheeks.

I glanced at Mary (she insisted I call her by her first name), who was softly crying.

Robert spoke again, *"Our pastor could not give us good reason, Chaplain; we are hoping you can. Can you?*

This question was neither new nor surprising to me. It was a very normal and valid question. I had heard the *"why?"* question from many different patients, all who believed they were justified in asking the same question. Some believed they were being 'punished' by God.

Others simply shook their head and could not believe that the life-limiting illness was happening to them.

For those devoutly dedicated to their faith, and faithful in following God, and conscientious as to how they lived their lives, it was doubly confusing and difficult. The mind set of many of those so affected found great difficulty in understanding the 'why?' this was happening to them.

As previously stated, this is a very legitimate and valid question. Some lose their faith and say, *"Since I am a child of God why doesn't he protect me? Others accuse saying, He did not protect me. Why would he do this to me? I am mad at God. I don't want anything to do with God. I am sick of religion; it is a crutch for the weak."*

These type questions are very difficult, and often impossible, to answer satisfactorily.

The book of Job, in the Old Testament, says *"that God rains on the just and the unjust,"* but this is not always easy to comprehend and accept.

Some terminally ill patients stop believing in God. Others grow closer to him. It appears when a life threatening illness is diagnosed, everything in the life experience is accelerated.

I asked Robert what his pastor told him in response to his question.

"He didn't have an answer. I was disappointed, I thought he could have done better," he responded, and continued, *"What do you say, Chaplain?"*

"I want to be very honest and frank with you, Robert," I began, and admitted, *"I don't know why bad things happen to good people. But I do know this. As a Christian, God tells us he will '...never leaves us nor forsakes us,'* Hebrews 13:5. *So I am confident, that whatever bad things happens to me, personally, even if I don't think I caused it, is not attributable to God.*

Sometimes we are victims of circumstances, and we can't control those circumstances. That's how I believe.

"Now, let's talk about you. You are a Christian. You are one of God's kids. Let's think for a moment about God as your Heavenly Father, and you as one of his children. Let's compare that to you, as an earthly father, for your children. Would you ever do anything that would harm or hurt one of your children? What would your answer to that be?" I asked.

"Well, you already know my answer, Chaplain. Of course I would never do anything to harm or hurt one of my children," he replied.

"Thank you for your honesty, Robert. Just as you wouldn't do anything to harm or hurt one of your children, neither would God. Does that make any sense? I asked.

"Yes, Chaplain, that gives me a different perspective. You've helped me a lot," he admitted.

"Good," I said, and asked, *"Is there anything else you need to talk about today, Robert?"*

"Yes." he said, *"Mary and I haven't told our children yet. We are struggling to know how to tell them. Do you have any ideas, Chaplain?* He asked.

I turned to face Mary, who had been listening intently to our conversation, and asked.

"Mary, before I try to answer that question, do you have any ideas or thoughts on how to tell the children about Robert's illness?"

"No. I've been thinking about it, and Robert and I have been talking about it, but I don't have any ideas yet," She answered, and then said, *"I'll be interested in hearing your comments."*

I thought for a few minutes and then suggested, *"Why don't we go to the Lord in prayer and ask for his guidance and direction?* They both agreed. We held hands and prayed for providential leadership and divine guidance. We joined our voices in reciting the Our Father prayer.

After prayer I felt compelled to share my personal feelings: *"Robert, Mary, what I am going to say comes from my heart; it's what I would do if I were in your place. So you may not agree with my reasoning, and that's O.K."* I assured them.

It seems to me that it would be a good idea to have a family meeting. If you agree, I would suggest that you, do it after dinner when you are having dessert. Food is always a good equalizer. It would not then be just mom, dad, and children; rather, it would be a family sharing time. I would keep it simple with as few words as possible. I would call the children by name and then talk to them. For example I would say something like this:

Carrie, Calvin, we need to tell you that daddy is very sick, and he is going to become more sick. Please understand, that there is going to be some changes in the things we do. It is no one's fault that daddy is sick, and daddy is not mad at anyone. Daddy is going to be home from work more. So when he feels like it, he can spend more time with both of you. But sometimes he is not going to feel well at all and he won't be able to spend time with either of you. So when he is very sick please let him rest and sleep. Do you understand?"

I stopped talking to let them absorb and process the information I had shared.

Robert then spoke, *"That sounds like a good plan, Chaplain. What do you think, Mary?"* he asked turning to his wife.

"I think it sounds O.K. It lets us be honest with the children," she said.

To validate her statement I said, *"You are right, Mary. It lets you be honest and, at the same time, it lets the children know that daddy is sick"*

I continued with the validation, *"It's important not to give too* much information at first. Let them become aware that daddy is sick. Reinforce this information when possible,"* I suggested.

Robert and Mary thanked me for my visit, input, and prayers. They asked me to *"come back again."*

I gave each of them a big bear hug, shook their hands and exited the home.

I made twice weekly visits with Robert and Mary over the next month. They told me that they took my suggestion on how to tell the children and that everything went well.

They were pleased that Calvin and Carrie accepted the news about their daddy's sickness and talked about it to him, and remembered it in their prayers at night before they went to bed.

Robert's condition exacerbated and his disease progressed. He became increasingly lethargic and difficult for Mary to manage at home. He was ultimately transferred to a health care facility near his home. Fortunately, his health insurance through his work paid for room and board.

This was a tremendous relief for Mary who was financially destitute and receiving financial assistance from her parents.

On my last visit with him at the health care facility the charge nurse informed that Robert's kidneys had shut down totally and that he had slipped into a comma early on that morning. She told me that *"Mary was in his room sitting at his bedside."*

I walked down the hallway to his room and softly opened the door. Mary looked up as I knocked and entered the room. She started to get up but I told her *"Please stay where you are, Mary."* She managed a weak smile, and offered her hand in greeting.

I took her hand, gently squeezed it and asked, *"May I read some Scripture and say some prayers and give Robert an anointing with oil and a blessing."*

"Please do," she answered.

I spoke into Robert's ear, *"Robert, it's the Chaplain. I am here with Mary. I am going to read a Scripture from the Psalms, say some prayers, and give you an anointing and blessing."*

I held Robert's hand, read the 23rd Psalm, said a prayer, and reached for Mary's hand. We recited the Our Father prayer, after which I anointed his forehead with oil, and gave him a blessing.

I told Mary, *"I'm as close as your phone, please call me if needed,"* She said she would. I gave her a hug, shook her hand and quietly left the room.

A week after his transfer into the health care facility Robert's kidneys had failed, and totally shut down. His body absorbed dangerous bacterial toxins, resulting in sepsis. An exacerbation of the infection attacked his vital organs and caused his body to also shut down.

With Mary sitting at his bedside holding his hand, Robert quietly made a peaceful transition, from this life to the next.

CHAPTER 43

Help Me Find Them...

Ronald Hamilton met me at the door, extended his hand in greeting, and introduced himself. *"I'm Ronald Hamilton,"* he said, *"Call me Ron."*

I accepted his hand and he gave me a firm handshake. I introduced myself. *"I'm Curtis, the hospice Chaplain,"*

He held open the door and invited me in. We entered the dining room and he pulled out a chair at the table for me to sit. He sat across the table from me. To get the conversation started I spoke first.

"How can I help?" I asked.

"It's a long story, Chaplain..." he began, and then stopped talking.

With a smile and a touch of humor I said, *"Sometimes it's not such a long story Ron, it's just the way we tell it."*

He picked up on the humor, laughed, and said, *"You are probably right. But it is, and has been a long story. I really don't know where to begin."*

"Start anywhere, Ron. The events and story you want to tell don't have to be in chronological order," I said, trying to encourage him to open up.

He thought for a moment and then began to talk: *"I'm a Viet Name Vet, chaplain I spent four and a half years in that hell hole. But one good thing happened to me while I was there. I met and fell in love with a beautiful 18 year old Vietnamese girl. We were just kids. Obviously, we didn't have a lot of time to spend together.*

I was 19 years old; a translator for the U. S. Army. After I was drafted, and finished recruit training, they asked for volunteers to learn the Vietnamese language. I volunteered."

"After my training I was assigned to an Intelligence company and shipped to Viet Nam. I had been interpretation for captured P.O.W.'s (prisoners of war) for about six months. It was very stressful work. I was granted some time off for R. and R (rest and relaxation). I went to Saigon (now Ho Chi Minh City) with some other GI's; we were having a few drinks in the bar when this beautiful girl came out carrying a basket of flowers. She approached us trying to sell us some flowers. I began talking with her in her own language. I learned her father was the owner of the bar. He heard us talking and came out to see who she was talking with. I introduced myself and then the mother came out to meet me.

"They seemed to like me at once. One thing led to another and after several times of meeting them they invited me to their home for dinner. I gladly accepted. The girl's name was Anh Thu. She seemed very shy at first, bur as we got to know one another she seemed to really like me. It was love at first sight for us. The more I was around her; the more I fell in love with her. I asked if she would marry me, and she said 'Yes, if my father approves.'

"I asked her father, and to my surprise he gave his approval. He had just one daughter and six sons; it was a large family. He was afraid that he might be captured by the North Vietnamese if they won over South Viet Nam, so he wanted someone to look after his daughter, wife and sons if he was captured and placed in a prisoner work, rehabilitation camp. I'm sure that is why he gave his permission.

"I went to my CO (commanding officer) and tried to obtain permission to get married on the base. He discouraged me by saying, 'It's not a good idea, because we never know what's going to happen in time of war, and that, it was an impossible request.'

"I went to the Chaplain and he agreed with the CO. He told me to tell her that when I return to the United States I would send for her."

"I shared with An Thu what the military Chaplain had said. I called her, at her father's bar and told her the bad news. We were both disappointed but she understood. I assured her, as soon as I got back home, I would immediately start the process of making it legal, for her to join me in the United States, at which time we would be married.

I could hear tears in her voice. She said, 'I hope so, because I am pregnant.' She was elated, and I was excited; I was going to be a father!"

"I wanted to see her again, but that was impossible. I had already used up all of my R. and R.(rest and relaxation) time. I told her how sorry I was that we couldn't get married, but I again assured her that I would send for her just as soon as I was returned to the United States. I didn't want to say good-bye but I had to go. A new group of P.O W.'s had been captured and I was scheduled to translate the interrogation process.

"Shortly after that, my outfit was transferred to another war zone. I tried to stay in touch with An Thu, but I was never able to re-connect with her by telephone.

"Abruptly, with a change of administration at the White House, word came down that we were 'going home.'" I immediately went to my C.O and asked how I could start the process for my pregnant girlfriend to immigrate to the U.S. He told me that 'it would not be possible,' at that time, and suggested I 'wait until I was back in the States to start the paperwork. 'I tried again to get in touch with An Thu, to no avail. I wrote her a letter explaining what had happened and gave her my address in the United States; I never heard from her again.

"My division returned to the U.S. and, as soon as possible, I went to the U.S Embassy. I explained my situation and tried to get the paperwork started. I was told 'the Embassy would necessarily' have to *'locate her before they could start processing any paperwork' and, that they would need confirmation from her, that she was, in fact, pregnant with my child.'*

"*For a month I patiently waited to hear from them, with reference to the information I had given them, to tell me They had located her. When I did hear from them, it was bad news.*

"*They told me that they 'could not locate An Thu.' And that, 'there was no way they could help me' because, she 'had such a common name, that there were hundreds of thousands of Viet Nam female residents who had the same name.'*

"*So you see, Chaplain, why I said it was such a long story. For the past 32 years I have been trying to locate the woman whom I want as my wife, and the child she bore me, without success. I don't understand what could have happened to her. If she is still alive, she could have contacted me, and gotten in touch with me. She had my address in the U.S, and I have never moved since I came home from Viet Nam. I have asked for help from the Red Cross, the United Way, and the VFW (Veterans of Foreign Wars,) and other agencies, but none have been able to find her. Do you think you can you help me, Chaplain?*" he asked, tears filling his eyes.

I am rarely at a loss for words, but right then I was. Finally, I was able to comment, "*I'll see what can be done.*"

This was all new information to me. My notification contained only medical data and history. This was personal. The medical record I had reviewed stated he had recently been diagnosed with end stage lung cancer; a terminal illness. And that, he was a 54 year old male Caucasian, and that, he had been referred to hospice. As a veteran Ron Hamilton was eligible for veteran's benefits, but had opted to go with a private hospice agency rather than the VA hospital, because he was also Medicare eligible.

I really wanted to go the extra mile and help Ron. He had sacrificed his youth in going to war in Viet Nam. I felt the least that could be done, was to try and assist him, in locating his long lost girlfriend and the mother of his child, he had never seen.

Contact was made with a local state senator regarding Ron's situation. There was an immediate response with a request for additional information. The information which had been provided by Ron was forwarded.

The senator got the Veteran's Administration, State Department, and Defense Department involved in the search for Ron's long, lost family. Unfortunately, after exhaustive searching of all available avenues the news was not good. It was reported by all agencies that no success was obtained in locating them.

By the time the search ended Ron's disease had progressed. He told me, at one of our last meetings that he was coughing up blood daily, and that there was nothing that could be done except keep his pain under control with pain medication in an attempt to keep him free from pain and comfortable.

Ron's body had deteriorated and he was very cachectic, almost to the point of skin and bone. I hated to tell him the bad news that could possibly cause his condition to be further exacerbated; an exhaustive search of available records failed to identify and find *An Thu* his wartime lover, and mother of a child he had never seen.

Ron had one only living relative. An older brother George, who lived out of state, who was also experiencing health issues with his heart and chronic obstructive pulmonary disease (COPD). Ron had told me that he didn't even want George to know about his illness fearing that it would cause his brother's health to get worse. Therefore, I had to be the one to be the bearer of bad news for both Ron and George.

I called the health care facility where he had been placed due to the deteriorating condition and talked to the charge nurse. She reported that his condition was worsening, that he had stopped eating, and was having decreased alertness with increased weakness.

I notified the Social Worker was assigned to his case to see if she could make a joint visit with me, thinking that another person present would soften the disappointing news. She agreed.

We scheduled a time together so that we both could visit Ron.

Upon arrival we conferred with the charge nurse who reported *"no concerns at this time."*

She confirmed what we had already heard; *"the patient is not doing too well."*

Ron was lying on his back using oxygen continuously with a nasal candela. He looked up as we entered his room and managed a weak smile. His condition had changed remarkably since my last visit. He appeared to have lost even more weight. His hospital gown seemed to just hang on his emaciated frame.

I offered my hand in greeting; he slowly reached out his hand. His limp hand shake further evidence of his weakened condition.

The social worker Alma squeezed his shoulder and placed a hand on his forehead. She said *"You are hot to the touch;"* and asked, *"Ron, do you feel hot?"*

He nodded his head. Alma moistened a wash cloth in ice-cold water and placed it across his forehead as a cooling measure. He mouthed the words *"Thank you,"* and then in a whisper said, *"That feels good,"* his voice was raspy and he struggled to project.

To make him as comfortable as possible I pulled a chair close to his bed. Just then the primary care physician Dr. Lang entered the room. We knew one another, and greeted each other. Then both the social worker and I stood aside to the side deferring to Dr. Lang's medical visit.

We observed Dr. Lang place a stethoscope and listen to Ron's heart, and then took his blood pressure, after which he said to him *"Hang in there,"* and left the room.

I followed the doctor into the hallway and requested a report on Ron's condition.

"What's his condition, Dr. Lang?" I asked.

"Ron is failing fast. He has a respiratory rattle (commonly called a death rattle) *and is probably transitioning into death."* He went on to say, *"It's doubtful that he will make it through the night, Chaplain. Better notify the family, if he has family members,"* the doctor shook my hand, said *"Keep up the good work, Reverend,"* and disappeared down the hall of the health care facility.

After the doctor left I conferred with Alma the Social Worker as to whether or not we should attempt to tell Ron the bad news about not being able to find his long lost soul mate. After serious consideration and discussion we agreed *not to* tell him. Our reasoning was, it would be better not to tell him, than have him die with a heavier and broken heart.

Satisfied with our decision, we went back into Ron's room. He lay on his back and had his eyes closed. It appeared as if he had stopped breathing. We had to observe him very closely to see if he was, in fact, breathing. There appeared to be a very slight raising and lowering of the chest.

I moved along side of him and spoke into his ear. "Ron, it's the Chaplain. I am here with Alma the Social Worker. I would like to say some prayers with you." There was no response. I took his hand and held it, I again spoke into his ear. *"Ron, if you can hear me, please squeeze my hand."* I sensed a very faint movement of the hand.

"Good," I said into his ear, *"That's good. I felt your squeeze. Is it O.K. to pray with you?"* I asked. I waited a few seconds and again thought I sensed an even fainter movement. It was difficult to know for sure; the movement had seemed almost indiscernible.

I said some prayers, asking God to let Ron be free from pain and comfortable. Alma and I joined our voices in reciting the Our Father prayer. I then anointed him with oil and gave him a blessing.

I spoke into Ron's ear, *"Ron, if we don't see you again here on planet earth, we will see you one day in heaven."*

That comment seemed so inadequate; so incomplete. I thought for a few moments and then decided to add to the statement.

"Ron, when you get to Heaven you will once again find your soul mate, An Thu."

I had continued to hold his hand, and I felt what I perceived to be the faintest of movement; I chose to believe, the slight movement was his agreement.

I learned the next day that, in a peaceful sleep, at approximately 6:45 PM that same evening, Ron passed from this life to the next.

CHAPTER 44

I Thought it Only Happened to Women

James Scott was a retired long distance, semi-truck driver. For thirty five years he had driven over the road from Los Angeles to St. Louis, and more recently from Los Angles to Vegas and back.

I first met Jim, as he liked to be called, after he became a hospice patient with the agency where I serve as Chaplain. During the onset of his service he had requested to see a *"non-denominational Chaplain."*

I stood on the porch of the mobile home where he and his wife Lee lived. I rang the bell for the second time and waited. I noticed someone pull aside a curtain and peer out, then momentarily opened the door.

A tall, attractive woman asked, *"Are you the Chaplain?"*

"Yes," I replied. *"My name is Chaplain Curtis. I have an appointment with Mr. Scott."*

"Yes," she answered, and extended her hand in greeting, *"I'm Lee, his wife. Please come in, Chaplain. Jim is in the living room."*

I entered the home and followed her through the kitchen, dining room and into the living room. Mr. Scott _ Jim, he insisted on being called _ sat in a rocker-recliner watching television. I approached him, offered my hand in greeting, and introduced myself, *"I'm Curtis, the Hospice Chaplain."*

He accepted my hand, gave it a friendly grip and said, *"I'm Jim Scott. I'm pleased to meet you."*

"I am please you requested my service, Mr. Scott..." He interrupted me, *"Call me Jim, Chaplain,"* he invited.

"I began again, *"I'm pleased you asked to see me,*

"I really needed to talk with you about some things," he said.

"Good, I am a good listener," I told him. *While you are thinking about what you want to say, let me ask, how are you getting along?"*

"I don't know: angry, confused and scared, for sure," he said.

"Which one of those issues would you like to talk about," I asked.

He thought for a few minutes and then said, *"Let's talk about the confusion." "O.K., how are you confused?" I asked.*

"Chaplain, I've always heard that women are the only ones who get breast cancer, but that's what my doctor told me I have. I've had this lump on my chest, just over my heart, for a while. I thought it was from hitting my chest against the steering wheel of my truck when I had a fender bender accident about six months ago. But it didn't go away. I went to my family doctor who referred me to an oncologist. The oncologist took x-rays, and then did a biopsy. He determined that I had breast cancer. I am so embarrassed. The left side of my chest swelled up so that I have a breast and looked like a woman..." his voice broke with emotion; he stopped talking.

He looked at me and I could see his eyes brimming with tears. He continued, *"Look at me, I'm a rough and rugged truck driver. I'm supposed to be macho, and here am about to cry like a baby."*

I attempted to empathize and validate his concern by saying, *"Ron, cancer is no respecter of persons. It attacks male and female alike. Cancer is a malignant growth of cells in our body that invades tissue and interferes with the functioning of the part that is affected. It is certainly nothing to be embarrassed about,"* I assured him

"I wanted them to operate, Chaplain but the oncologist told me

that it had spread to the lymph nodes, and that surgery would not do any good. So I guess I'm a goner," he sadly said.

"What did the doctor tell you about your illness?" I asked.

"He said I have less than a year to live, so get my affairs in order," he answered; again, his voice broke and he became emotional.

"You requested to see me, Jim. How can I help?" I asked.

"I don't know, Chaplain, I'm just feeling overwhelmed. I needed someone to talk to for some spiritual guidance," he replied.

"What does that mean?" I asked, trying to determine an avenue for discussion.

"Well, I'm a believer and I used to be religious but not lately. Being a long haul truck driver I never knew what city I would be in on Sunday. I put my church attendance on hold. I haven't been to church in years," he told me.

"What about your family? Is your wife and children church connected?" I asked.

"My wife goes to a small Baptist church occasionally. I don't know about my son and daughter," he answered.

"Would you feel comfortable talking to your wife's pastor?" I asked.

"I don't know. I have never met him," he replied.

"Jim, I'm not trying to tell you what to do, but may I make a suggestion?" I asked.

"Sure, go ahead," he invited.

"May I suggest that you start attending church with your wife, meet and become acquainted with the pastor, then request an appointment with him to talk about your religious life experiences?" I suggested.

"That's a good idea," he agreed, and continued, *"We could do that this Sunday."* I asked if there was anything else I could help him with and he said, *"Not that I can think of."*

"What about your anger, and being scared?" I reminded him of his previous statement.

"Well, I'm angry, but not at anyone in particular, I'm just angry

that my life is being cut short by a disease I have no control over. Again, I'm not mad at anyone; just mad," he replied.

"Understandably so," I agreed with him. *"What about being scared,"* I asked.

He said, *"I'm scared because I don't know if I'm going to have a lot of pain, or if my dying is going to take a long time, or what. You might say I'm scared of the unknown."*

"Those are very normal, valid concerns and fears, Jim. Probably no one knows exactly how to deal with the unknown, especially when it comes to illness that will result in death. Facing death is a scary thing. But the one thing I do know is, that we can deal with it one day at a time."

"There is an old saying I learned as a child in Sunday School, Jim, that says: "One day at a time; one thing at a time, trusting God all of the time. That works for the believer, and Jim, you said you are a believer. I am also a believer, and it works for me," I said, sharing my spiritual philosophy.

I sensed that he was getting tired from all the conversation so I started bringing the visit to a close.

"May I come see you again?" I asked.

"Sure Chaplain, anytime; you've helped me a lot today," he replied.

"May I say some prayers with you before I leave?" I asked.

"Please do," he invited.

I said some prayers, asking God to help him with his plan to go to church with his wife. Further, that an opportunity would open up so he could make an appointment with the pastor to discuss his spiritual issues. I then asked God to keep him free from pain and comfortable, and to grant unto him the desires of his heart.

He thanked me for my visit and my prayers. He walked to the door with me, shook my hand, and said, *"Chaplain, you are welcome anytime.*

I told him, *"I will see you, when I see you. Bye for now."*

He stood on the porch and waved as I drove out of sight.

On follow-up visits Jim told me that he had visited his wife Lee's church, and had met and counseled with the pastor. He told me that after attending for several Sunday's both he and wife Lee joined the church, along with their adult children, who also lived in the area.

Jim appeared to be much calmer and more accepting of his illness.

Jim and I had weekly visit for the next two months. On one of our last visit I observed that his disease had progressed and metastasized to both sides of his chest. The pain had increased and was being controlled by pain medication treatments.

He had lost weight and it was obvious that his already compromised physical condition was deteriorating his body. His 6 foot 8 inch frame had become remarkably emaciated.

By his own admission he said, *"I've lost my appetite, and I'm as weak as a kitten."* I asked about his re-connection with the church.

"Chaplain, I re-newed my vows of faith and re-dedicated my life to the Lord. Pastor Ron has been calling every day, and dropping by once a week," he said.

"Good. I'm pleased you are receiving strong spiritual support," I told him.

"Thanks to you, Chaplain," he said, complimenting me.

"No. Not at all, Jim. It was your decision" I assured him.

"Well, I'm giving you the credit, anyway," he said.

"I decline; let's give God the credit," I said with a smile.

"I'll go for that." he agreed.

I sensed he was getting tired, so I began bringing my visit to a close.

"May I pray with you before I leave?" I asked.

"Absolutely, wouldn't have it any other way," he said.

I held his hand, said some prayers, anointed him with oil, and gave him a blessing.

He was having difficulty holding his eyelids open, and was nodding off." *Thanks for seeing me today, Jim. May I come see you again?"* I asked.

He seemed to awaken with a start, *nodded* his head and shook my hand and said, *"Yes. By all means, Chaplain."*

This was on Friday in the late afternoon. Monday morning I learned that over the week-end Jim's condition had worsened, and that his primary care giver and wife Lee, was exhausted due to his pain becoming uncontrollable.

He was transferred to a health care facility for continuous care, due to pain out of control.

Jim's condition continued to deteriorate. He became incontinent of bladder and bowl, and his pain continued to exacerbate out of control. His status was changed to crisis care with a 24 hour nurse present to monitor his medications and to bring the pain under control.

On Wednesday, he slipped into a comma and never awakened; he appeared to be actively dying.

The wife, family, and pastor were notified. They arrived, and began an around-the-clock prayer vigil for his comfort, spiritual support, and peaceful death.

Surrounded by wife Lee, son, daughter, and new pastor Ron, on Thursday morning, at 12:33 A.M. James, "Jim" Scott stopped breathing.

CHAPTER 45

O.K., O.K.!

"Young Sik Noh spoke to me in broken English, with a Korean accent.

"I'm Christian, I love God," he said, when I asked on the phone if he wanted to talk to a Christian Chaplain.

"I understand, Mr. Noh. I'm asking if you want to see me. I'm a Christian Chaplain," I told him.

"O.K., O.K.! I see you," he answered.

"I'll see you today," I told him.

"O.K., O.K.!" he said again.

His medical records stated that he had a diagnosis of lung cancer. He had been referred to the hospice agency where I serve as chaplain.

I arrived at the senior center where he was a resident. The door was opened by an attractive Korean lady who spoke fluent English. She identified herself.

"I'm *Kim, Young Sik's wife, she said."*

"My name is Curtis. I'm the hospice Chaplain," I said, introducing myself.

"Oh, thank you for coming, Chaplain," she answered, and showed me into the living room.

A man sat on the sofa. He arose, walked across the room, and bowed to me.

"Chaplain, this is my husband, Young Sik," she said.

"I'm Christian," the man smiled, and bowed again, and shook my hand.

He bowed again and made a motion toward the sofa inviting me to sit. I accepted the invitation and sat down.

I looked at wife Kim and asked, *"Will you translate for me?"*

She smiled agreement and, at the same time, and nodded her head.

I asked her to provide some family history, which would enable me to be of greater service.

She turned and spoke to Young Sik in Korean. He replied in Korean, nodding his head and looking at me. I presumed she had asked permission to share the requested information.

HIS STORY AS TOLD BY WIFE KIM:

Young Sik's older brother and his aging parents immigrated to the United States five years ago so his father could have rare heart surgery by American surgeons. The operation was a success but his father passed away a year later. His mother Sugi, was left alone when his brother was killed in an auto accident.

Young Sik made a decision to come to the US to care for his widowed mother. Due to the loss of his father, and brother, and the added responsibility of caring for his mother, in trying to work to earn enough money to live on, he started smoking excessively. He developed bronchitis, and eventually emphysema which went untreated.

The recent death of his mother caused deep bereavement, grief, and sadness. The increased stress caused him to start smoking three packs of cigarettes a day. He began coughing up blood and finally went to a doctor who diagnosed him with the terminal disease of lung cancer.

Kim stopped, looked at Young Sik and smiled. He returned her smile. She continued his story.

Young Sik was able to continue living in the senior center because he was over 55 years of age, because both parents had lived there, and because of Young Sik's limited income he was eligible and qualified for residency.

Kim then shared some information about her and Young Sik Noh. She said, *"I'm a business woman. In Korea, I own a clothing manufacturing business that makes ladies clothing."*

"I travel all over the world negotiating contracts to supply ladies fashionable clothing to retail outlets for resale. I work with some very large companies in the US.

"Young Sik and I agreed that it would be best for him to come to America to take care of his mother Sogi, rather than bring her back to Korea. I try to spend as much time as possible with Young Sik when I travel to the United States."

She stopped talking and said, *"That is as much as I know about the situation, other than I now know that he has been diagnosed with a terminal illness of lung cancer."* She then asked,

"Is there anything else you need to know, Chaplain?"

"No," I replied, *"you have given me important and valuable information. Thank you."* I then asked, Can you please ask Young Sik how I, as a Christian Chaplain, can help him?"

She again turned to Young Sik and spoke in Korean. Surprisingly, he answered in English.

"Church-e," he said, *"I want church-e."*

Kim turned to me and said, *"Young Sik wants to be put in touch with a Christian Korean speaking church, Chaplain. He wants to get closer to God in this tragic time in his life."*

"Good," I said. *"Tell him I will help him to find a local Christian Korean speaking church, and have the pastor contact him."*

She turned to Young Sik and translated what I had said.

He looked at me, smiled, bowed and said, *"Thank you, thank you."*

I asked if there was anything else I could do, and Kim said, *"You will have done enough if you can locate a church for Young Sik."*

I suggested I close my visit with a prayer. She smiled, nodded and reached for Young Sik's hand. We bowed our heads and prayed together.

I shook both Kim's and Young Sik's hand, and bowed to them. They smiled and returned my bow.

I told them, *"I will see you again, soon."*

He said, *"O.K., O.K."*

I gave Kim my business card, after jotting down my cell phone number on it.

"Please feel free to call me anytime," I said, encouraging her to stay in touch.

"I will let you know whenever I am in town and visit with you and Young Sik," she said. I thanked her and left the building.

In the following week I was able to contact a Christian Korean church in the area. The pastor agreed to visit Young Sik and even provide transportation, by the church, to the church from the senior center, and back to the senior center after church.

I was able to connect with the wife Kim and give her the good news. She told me that she would call Young Sik and let him know the pastor would call him. She was very pleased, and thanked me profusely.

On follow up visits I was able to see Young Sik and wife Kim several more times.

The last time I visited with him at the senior center he had changed remarkably. Due to his deteriorating condition the hospice agency had changed his status from routine to critical care. His increased pain and deteriorating condition dictated a 24 hour nurse assigned to monitor his level of pain and overall comfort care. He was minimally responsive and appeared to be very lethargic.

I spoke into his ear, and called his name. He momentarily aroused, opened his eyes, smiled at me, and then slid back into sleep.

The critical care nurse told me that the wife Kim had been called and was going to be arriving later in the evening.

"Have Kim call me if she needs to talk," I said to the critical care nurse, and left the building.

I later learned that Kim had arrived just before Young Sik slipped into a comma.

It appeared as if time had been provided, by a Higher Power, for a "Christian" man to say good bye to his faithful wife.

Friday the 13th. Of July, wife Kim at his bedside, with a peaceful death Young Sik Noh passed into eternity.

CHAPTER 46

I'm Losing My Voice...

B rian Altman was 48 years old. He was a construction foreman working on major construction projects building bridges, freeways and highways. At his invitation I sat in his living room listening to his story.

A better word would be "reading" his story. Brian had been diagnosed with laryngeal cancer and he had lost his ability to communicate with voice. He was communicating with a word processor and a computer monitor. It was really quite ingenious: a friend of Brian's was a computer technician and had rigged up a 21" monitor screen to a computer word processor keyboard and had increased the font to a much larger size.

It appeared to be easy for Brian to use. It was certainly easy to read, and to communicate with him verbally, in response to his written messages, because there was nothing wrong with his hearing.

Brian wrote that he was *"Divorced and the father of an adult son who lived in his home. He was out of town at the time of my visit. He was following in his father's footsteps and working in construction"*. It was easy to keep up with Brian's computer monitor as he was writing.

He wrote, *"My problem started with a sore throat. I just thought it was from too many cigarettes, so I tapered off my smoking, bought some penicillin lozenges and it seemed to get better; I never went to a doctor."*

I finished reading his message and asked him to continue.

"The next time my throat started hurting I lost my voice for a couple of days," he wrote. At my nod, he continued typing. *"Now, I'm starting to get worried."*

"I had almost stopped smoking, so I knew it was not from cigarettes. I then found a lump in my throat. So I scheduled an appointment with my doctor

He took a biopsy and two weeks later told me that it was a cancerous growth, and wanted to start chemotherapy right away. I wasn't so sure I wanted any chemo treatments, and by this time I was starting to have difficulty swallowing, and I was again losing my voice.

"I finally agreed to chemo. I had to quit my construction work. My body felt like it was falling apart. I lost my appetite and become so weak I could hardly walk across the living room.

All I wanted to do was sleep. I started losing weight, along with my hair. My doctor said I have between three to six months to live. That's where I'm at, Chaplain." he finished typing and waited until I caught up reading the message.

"How can I help?" I asked.

He thought for a few minutes and then began typing another message.

"Chaplain, I need to get right with God. I was brought up a Methodist but I dropped out of church when I started working in construction. I was out of town a lot, and at the end of the day was too tired to try and find a church and get up and go." He stopped typing.

I finished reading the monitor and nodded that I understood his question.

"What can I do to get right with God?" he typed.

"Are you still in touch with your family; your parents?" I asked.

He nodded, *"Yes."*

"Do they still attend church?" I asked.

"Yes," he nodded again.

"Why don't you make plans to attend church with them, and then communicate with their pastor. He will be able to guide you in re-newing your vows of faith in God, and re-dedicating your life," I suggested.

"That's a good idea, Chaplain. Why didn't I think of that? I'll do it!" he typed smiling.

"That's why I am here, Brian, to help you sort out things," I replied laughing.

Brian appeared anxious to drive to his parents to make the church attendance arrangements. I sensed his restlessness and began to end my visit.

"I'm going to leave now, Brian," I told him, *"But I'd like to come back and see you again. May I?"* I asked.

"Yes! Yes! Yes!" he typed. I thanked him for the visit, shook his hand and said, *"so long for now."*

In subsequent visits I felt like I gained strong rapport with Brian. He told me via word processor and computer screen that he had made arrangements to attend church with his parents. He had re-newed his vows of faith in God and, as a result, had reconciled with his ex-wife who had re-married.

He typed, *"We are friends again."*

Brian's disease progressed. His physical condition deteriorated rapidly. A 24 hour live-in caregiver was hired by his parents to provide for his comfort care and every day needs.

During my last visit with him he handed me a typewritten note.

"I want you to do my funeral, Chaplain, if you will. I have prepared this information for you to use," I read his message and turned to the second page on which he had prepared information to be used at the funeral memorial service.

"I consider it an honor, Brian," I assured him agreeing to conduct his funeral memorial.

He appeared pale and lethargic. Sensing his tiredness I asked, *"May I pray with you, and give you an anointing and blessing?"*

He nodded his consent.

Following the prayer I said: *"Brian, I'm pleased that you were able to complete some unfinished business with God."*

Suddenly, his face glowed with a radiance I had not seen before. His eyes shined brightly through the tears. He held my hand and mouthed the words, *"Thank you."*

I squeezed his hand and said, *"You are very welcome,"* and told him, *"If I don't see you again here on planet earth, I will see you one day in Heaven."*

His smile seemed to make the room brighter. I softly opened the door, quietly left the room and stepped into the hallway.

I was met by the caregiver who silently led me down the hallway and out of the home.

The next day I learned that Brian Altman had peacefully went to sleep and never awakened that very evening.

At his funeral I voiced a statement clearly reflecting my personal opinion of Brian:

"Today, Brian's spirit rests and abides in that place eternal in the heavens, that place not made with hands, called paradise."

CHAPTER 47

I'm Feeling Guilty

The patient was 78 years old, male Caucasian. His name was Carl Jensen. And he had recently been diagnosed with colon cancer. In addition to his terminal illness he had many accompanying ailments and accidents. His medical record stated that he had sustained a fall and fractured his left hip six months prior to his cancer diagnosis.

A year prior to that he had experienced a cardio vascular accident (CVA) also known as a stroke which had impaired the use of the right side of his body.

At the onset of his hospice start of care service he had expressed a desire to see a chaplain for spiritual counsel and support.

I entered his room at the health care facility, where he was a resident. I introduced myself and asked, *"How are you getting along, Mr. Jensen?"*

"Not very good," he answered, and said, *"Call me Sarge that was my rank in the Army."*

"Want to talk about it?" I invited.

"Not much to talk about," he replied.

"I'm a good listener. Why don't you start anywhere," I encouraged.

"I've been having a lot of pain, Chaplain," he said.

He had been admitted to the hospice agency under general inpatient status for pain out of control and family crisis.

"Are you having pain right now?" I asked.

"No. No pain," he assured me.

"How can I be of help, Sarge?" I asked.

"I'm not sure. Just pray for me, I guess," he replied.

"What is your religious preference?" I asked.

"I'm Protestant; Christian you could say," he said.

"Any denomination?" I queried.

"No, just Christian," he replied.

"Are you connected to a particular Christian church?" I asked.

"No, not since I was a young man," he said.

"Would you like to see a minister from one of the local Christian churches?" I asked him.

"No. No need to; it wouldn't do any good," he said.

"Do you need to talk about anything that may be troubling you?" I asked trying to develop rapport and at the same time determine an avenue for discussion.

"No. Not that I know of..." he began and then stopped talking in mid-sentence. He then started again, just where he left off.

"There is something on my mind," he informed me.

"Do you want to share your concerns?" I encouraged.

"Yes, I do," he said, then continued, *"Is this going to be confidential"* he asked.

I assured him it was patient, clergy privileged communication, and that it was strictly confidential.

"Good, this is very personal information. I'm still grieving my late wife who died twenty years ago. No," he corrected himself, *"it's more than that; I'm feeling guilty,"* he said.

"Why do you feel guilty?" I asked, encouraging him to open up and talk about it.

"I was in the military, being transferred here, there and everywhere. That was O.K. until I was ordered overseas. My wife and family could not go with me to the duty stations. So we had to maintain separate residences.

"I was away from home; I was a heavy drinker. My wife Sally

had been diagnosed with cardiomyopathy. She told me it was too much for her to try and be mother, father and disciplinarian for our kids. As a result of being separated my wife told me that she 'wanted a divorce.'

"In addition to our marital problems, our oldest daughter Carla started drinking, staying out all night, and doing drugs. My wife blamed me for that, because I was always an 'absent father.' The daughter finally ran away from home and stopped talking to us. We didn't even know where she was, until we received a call from the police department that she had committed suicide.

"The wife fell apart, she said 'it was all my fault for being an alcoholic; that I had been a bad influence in our daughter Carla's life.'" In the meantime, I finished a tour of duty overseas and was reassigned to the states. I took a thirty day furlough.

He stopped talking, pausing in life review and then continued.

"This was all too much for Sally. She filed for divorce. That hit me like a ton of bricks. I tried to talk her out of the divorce, but she said 'I've had it!' What was I to do?

I stayed in contact with her and provided money for her and Gail, the youngest daughter, paid their rent, utilities, and groceries. I kept trying to convince her to take me back, and we were almost reconciled. I thought we were going back together."

"My furlough was up so I had to go back to active duty. I had no sooner arrived at my new base when I received an emergency call from Gail, that Sally was in the hospital with a stroke. I applied for, and received, an emergency family medical leave. I went to their apartment, picked up daughter Gail, and drove to the hospital.

"The doctor conferenced with me, and said that, Sally had sustained a minor stroke, with minimal residual damage, and that she 'should make a full recovery.'

Upon her discharge, from the hospital, Gail and I were able to get her back home. I thought everything was going to be O.K. Sally had agreed to take me back, and to re-marry me. I was feeling pretty *good. My emergency family leave time was up so I had to report back to the base.*

"Things appeared to be going well. About a month later I received another emergency call from Gail. Sally had overdosed on prescription drugs and the paramedics were not able to resuscitate her.

"The coroner ruled Sally's death 'an accidental over dose,' but I'm not so sure. I've thought about it a lot, and I think she committed suicide, and I feel responsible; on top of everything else my disease. And now, Chaplain my terminal illness.

"This presents another difficult situation. My daughter Gail has always been able to turn to me when she needed advice or help. But now that I am sick she doesn't have anyone to turn to for support; she has no one else.

"Gail has two teen-age sons _ my grandkids _ who are absolutely no help to her. She says they are 'getting out of control.'"

Sarge stopped talking and asked, *"Have I bent your ear far enough, Chaplain, with my tale of woes, or would you like to hear more?"*

"Sarge, it sounds like you've had a lot of losses," I empathized.

"You got that right, Chaplain," he agreed, *'But here's the capper; my daughter Gail's husband has just told her he 'wants out of the marriage; he wants a divorce.'*

"I'm pleased you have confided in me Sarge. How can I be of help?" I asked.

"You can start by praying for me, my daughter Gail, my grandsons Mark and Mike," he responded.

"I will certainly be able to do that. Sounds like Gail could use some spiritual support. Would you want me to contact your daughter?" I asked.

"She might not return your call, but it would be worth trying." He answered.

"I will contact her and try to be of help in providing emotional and spiritual support," I told him.

Sarge thanked me and requested me to pray with him, and for his daughter and family.

"I will be pleased to pray with you, Sarge, I said," but before I pray, I need to ask, have ever forgiven yourself, for the blame you have accepted, concerning your daughter Cora and wife Sally's death?"

"I thought I had, Chaplain. I thought I had, but my illness brings it all back, and I'm not sure. I think I keep blaming myself for their deaths, thinking it could have been so different," he answered.

"Would you like to pray with me, asking God to help you re-enforce absolution for your self-blame, and to take away the emotional pain," I asked.

"Yes. I would like that," he said.

I told him that I was going to pray first, asking God to hear and answer his prayer concerning the issues he had shared. I then told him, after I complete my prayer, I will ask you to repeat after me another prayer, if the words express the desires of your heart.

"I will," he said.

With bowed head, I waited a few minutes in silent prayer asking God to give me meaningful words to use on Carl's behalf. I then began to pray.

THE PRAYER:

"Father, you know Carl's every need, even before we come to you in prayer on his behalf. You know he is struggling releasing the self-blame and responsibility of his daughter

Carol and wife Sally's death. We are aware that there is no time frame for bereavement, grief and sadness." "We also know that when we turn to you, that you can renew our strength and energy and help us to work through the bereavement process, and to see the side of death that you see when you tell us, 'there is rejoicing in the presence of the angels over the home going of one of your children,'

You tell us that, when we 'ask, we will receive.' On behalf of our new friend we ask that you hear and answer his prayers."

I then turned to Sarge and said, *"O.K., Sarge, now pray with me."*

"Heavenly Father, I pray right now that you will remove this burden of guilt I carry. Help me to accept responsibility for what I have control over in my life, and guide my thinking to know when I am not to blame, or responsible, for something that is not my fault. Forgive me for the things I have done, which I ought not to have done, and for the things which I have left undone. Direct my mind and my thinking, the words of my mouth and the meditations of my heart, that I might not sin against you. You are my rock and my salvation Help me to forgive myself. O, God, grant me the serenity to accept the things I cannot change, the courage to change the things I can, and the wisdom to know the difference. I pray in the name of our Lord and savior Jesus Christ. Amen

Sarge repeated every word with sincerity. After we said *"Amen"* he took a deep breath and said. *"I now feel much better, Chaplain."*

"I'm pleased to hear you say that," I answered, empathizing with him.

I sensed that it was time to leave, so I said, *"I'm going to leave now, Sarge. But remember, I am as close as your phone. Please don't hesitate to call me if needed,"* I invited.

"Thank you, Chaplain," and added, *"I will."*

I shook his hand and told him, *"I'll be pleased to see you again."*

"I hope so. Please visit anytime," he said.

I made attempts to get in touch with his daughter, but she never returned any of my telephone calls. I took her silence to mean that she didn't want any contact with the spiritual component, and that was O.K.

The cancer metastasized to Mr. Jensen's rectal area. Due to chronic constipation it caused great difficulty for him to have normal and regular bowel movements.

A week after my initial visit, I learned Carl Jensen had sustained a massive heart attack while attempting to have a bowel movement. He had collapsed, fallen out of a commode chair next to his bed, and died on the floor.

CHAPTER 48

It Was My Duty

According to the medical record, Frank Vandercam had been paralyzed from the waist down for 45 years. His paralysis had been cause by an auto accident. The spinal cord had been severely damaged. He had received extensive physical therapy, and psychotherapy following his accident.

The physical therapy had been ordered by his doctor to be used in an attempt to strengthen his spinal cord, and regain partial use of his lower extremities. And, in the event that the physical therapy was unsuccessful, the doctor had ordered psychotherapy to provide emotional coping skills.

Mr. Vandercam shared with me, that physical therapy had not been successful and, that he had learned to live an acceptable and normal life _ for him _ with his high school sweetheart Wilma, and wife of 36 years, who was now his constant companion and caregiver.

"She is my right hand, so to speak," he said.

Frank and Wilma had two adult sons Frank, Jr. and Fred, who lived out of town but visited frequently.

His wife continued to be his primary care giver, even though her sight was affected with glaucoma and was losing her vision. To make things more difficult she was no longer able to drive due to her failing eyesight, and subsequently, had to depend on friends or take a taxi during the week to attend to chores and to do light grocery and household shopping. Usually, one of the sons was available on the week-ends to help with major grocery store shopping and to run errands.

I stood at the side of his hospital bed placed in his bedroom. He motioned for me to sit He began to speak.

"It's good to see you, Chaplain. Thanks for coming. I've needed someone to talk to," he said.

"It's my pleasure to visit with you, Mr. Vandercam," I replied.

"Chaplain, call me Frank," he invited.

"I hope I can help; I'm a good listener," I told him.

"You have some time?" he asked.

"Sure. My time is your time," I assured him.

"I would like to bring you up to speed about my condition. Where I am today, if that's O.K.," he said.

I assured him it was fine and he began a life review.

"I'm a machinist by trade. I had my own machine shop and was doing quite well. I closed the shop one evening and was driving home. I got hit by a drunk driver. I was in a comma for two weeks and then woke up to find myself paralyzed from the waist down; a paraplegic. I was devastated. First, about my family. I had two small sons and a wife to support, and we had just bought a home. So I was very concerned about their welfare. Fortunately, the drunk driver had insurance and they stepped in to cover my huge medical expenses. I ultimately sued and received a small settlement, along with life-time medical benefits. But no amount of money could replace my health, or physical condition.

"My wife had to go to work. When I got well enough I set up a machine shop in my garage and took on small jobs. I was able to do that from a wheel chair, along with being a baby sitter for my kids, until they got old enough to go to school. I ran the shop out of the garage which provided a supplemental income. We are able to scrape by for fifteen years until my condition deteriorated, and my hands

and arms lost their strength. I couldn't hold on to anything. So I gave up being a machinist.

"I had to do something to fill my time so I started learning how to become a ham radio operator. I studied the rules and regulations and took the test. To my surprise I passed. My family pooled their resources and bought me a ham radio set. My sons installed a long-range antenna on the roof. Some of the neighbors objected, but when they found out I was a paraplegic, and that I was helping out the war effort, the complaints went away.

"In return, out of courtesy to the neighbors, I had my sons put an anti-static filter on the antenna so when I was using the ham radio it eliminated most interference on TV sets."

Frank paused for breath; I asked about a comment he had made.

"You mentioned that you were helping with the war effort. How did that happen?"

"World War two was going on. All ham radio operators were asked by the USO and Red Cross to transfer information between soldiers and their families. I volunteered to do this and spent hundreds of hours volunteering and relaying message information. It was the least I could do; it was my duty.

'That bring you up to date, Chaplain. You know the rest. I have been diagnosed with a terminal illness. A Central Nervous System disease (also known as CNS) they call it; and am now a hospice patient." he said.

Frank appeared to be very tired from all the energy he had used in verbalizing his life story.

"You appear to be tired, Frank. Do you want me to wind up my visit?" I asked.

"I am a little tired. Just let me catch my breath and I'll be O.K.," he said.

I sat in silence for several minutes, letting him recover his breath, then asked, *"What is your religious preference?"*

"I don't really have one. I am a nominal Christian. I've never been big on church, but I do believe in God," he answered.

"How can I be of help for you, Frank? I asked.

"Just by visiting with me and letting me talk," he said.

"I'll be pleased to do that," I told him.

"Good. You can say a prayer for me now," he invited.

I said a prayer with him ending with the Our Father prayer which he recited with me.

"I remember that prayer, I pray it every day," he said.

I asked if there was anything else I could do for him while I was there. He asked me to move a tray table which held a portable ham radio closer to the bed. He thanked me, turned on the radio, and started to communicate. He waved goodbye as he left the room.

"Come back and see me real soon," he said.

Frank and I had many more visits. He was a very intelligent and interesting man. He had a brilliant mind encapsulated in a non-responsive body.

He was very dependent upon his wife and often, she told me, was very demanding.

However, Wilma had learned to accept, and live with, his sometimes verbal abuse, and demanding demeanor.

Frank was bed bound and once a week a hired male care giver came to the home, got Frank up, and transferred him from bed to a wheel chair. He then pushed him into the kitchen and sat him at the table where he ate a delicious breakfast prepared by wife Wilma.

This was the highlight of Frank's week. It was one of the things he talked about every time I visited. He told me it was one of the few things he really looked forward to.

At subsequent visits it was obvious that Frank was changing. He had weighed over 300 pounds when he started hospice care and had lost 50 pounds in three months. He said he had *"Lost his appetite,"* and credited his weight loss to that.

However, I learned at an Interdisciplinary Meeting, from the RN Case Manager, that *"the progression of his disease was responsible for the weight loss,"* and that, *" his condition was deteriorating rapidly."*

At his request, my visits with Frank continued. At each visit he asked that I pray with him, for his wife Wilma, and for his family. His physical condition continued to decline. *"I have pain in every joint in my body,"* He told me. And that, *"The medicine did little to alleviate the pain."* He told me that, *"I requested the RN Case Manager to increase my pain medicine to my level of comfort"* and *"that she did that, but all I wanted to do was sleep, which was no good."* He continued, *"I would like to be awake and alert, but I have chosen the lesser of two alternatives; I want to be free from pain, so sleep here I come,"* he said sarcastically, and continued, *"Chaplain, when will I be free from this pain?"*

Frank was no longer able to be transferred from the bed to the wheel chair. This was a crushing blow to him. He had told me that it was *"one of the few things in life he had left to look forward to."*

Subsequently, his male care giver was no longer needed, thus, he had another loss in his life.

I decreased my visits from two times a week, to once a week, since each time I arrived he was resting and sleeping comfortably. I did not want to disturb him with the reasoning that he needed his rest more than he needed a repetitious visit from the Chaplain. When I did visit, if he was asleep, I spent the time being verbally supportive to his wife Wilma.

Frank's physical condition worsened, and went from bad to worse. The hospice agency changed his status to crisis care, with a 24 hour assigned nurse, providing care giver relief for Wilma.

The last time I visited with Frank, both the RN Case Manager and the Critical Care Nurse were present. They shared with me that Frank *"was actively dying."*

I asked if they had told Wilma. They said *"Yes. They had told her, and that she had notified the sons."*

Frank was no longer verbal, even when he awakened. He had eye contact with no apparent cognition, or recognition, and physically was non-responsive. He appeared to be in a persistent vegetative state, and showed no response to the calling of his name, or the squeezing of his hand.

I held his hand and said a brief prayer in his ear. I attempted to give some spiritual support to Wilma, gave her a hug, told her, *"I am as close as the phone if you need me,"* and let myself out of the home.

I was informed by the RN Case Manager that, Wilma, along with the Critical Care Nurse, stayed at Frank's bedside in an all-night vigil.

The next day I learned, at 4:50 PM that afternoon, Frank had made the transition from this life to the next.

When I heard of his passing I remembered his question from a previous visit.

"Chaplain, when will I be free from this pain?" As a post-answer to his question, the words of Martin Luther King sprang into my mind:

"Free at last, free at last; thank God I'm free at last."

The difference being, Frank was *"free,"* from a *different* kind of *bondage*; the *bondage of pain*.

CHAPTER 49

If There is a God

Kenneth Clark opened the door and asked, *"Who are you? And what do you want?"*

I smiled, presented a business card, and said, *"My name is Curtis. I'm the hospice Chaplain."*

"Oh," he said, *"I'm Clark; Kenneth Clark. Come on in."*

I stepped inside a well-kept home located in a Leisure World Senior Complex community, in Southern California. We walked into the living room and Mr. Clark motioned for me to sit on a sofa. He took a seat next to me.

He said. *"The reason I wanted to see you Chaplain was because I have some questions I need answers to."*

He asked about my credentials. My answers seemed to satisfy him.

"I hope I can answer your questions satisfactorily," I told him.

"Me, too," he replied, and began.

"I am a retired engineer, Chaplain. My philosophy in life, consistent with my engineering background, is 'an explanation for everything. Everything must fit into a design or plan, and everything must be able to make reasonable, intelligent sense,' he stopped talking and waited for my response.

"I'm following your reasoning, Dr. Clark, please go on," I invited.

He had told me he had a Ph.D. Degree in engineering, so I wanted to address him by his appropriate title. It was important for me to note that Dr. Kenneth Clark was well educated, with a Ph.D. degree in structural engineering, and had spent 35 years on a career track with the Lockheed Aircraft Company.

"I am 83 years old, and I have recently lost my wife of fifty years. She suffered with Alzheimer's for the last ten years.

Chaplain, my wife was very religious; Presbyterian. I'm an agnostic. What I don't understand in religion _ if there is a God _ why would a so called Higher Power of the universe cause, or permit pain and suffering to extend to humanity? My wife Clara suffered in a hell of anxiety and confusion, and suffering for over ten years, yet she was a strong believer , and went to church regularly."

"Dr. Clark, you have voiced an age old question: Why do bad things happen to good people? I joined in his questioning, and confirmed his reasoning.

"I guess you could say that," he answered, and then repeated the *"Why?"*

"Dr. Clark, I want to be as honest and straight forward as possible. I don't have the answer to that question. I don't know. But, from a spiritual perspective, I do know a logical and reasonable answer. For the non-believer in God, it is difficult to accept perspectives emanating from belief in, and faith in, a higher power. I do know this. God does not cause bad things to happen to good people. However, God does permit man to become a victim of his own self-made circumstances, or circumstances caused by world situations.

"It is my personal belief that diseases such as Alzheimer's, cancer, and others, is a direct result of the forces of evil; specifically Satan. To the non-believer this sounds like an Aesop Fable, but to the believer it is the gospel truth.

"In my opinion, it would be a direct contradiction of God's love for him to be personally responsible for any member of his creation to be so affected.

"Dr. Clark, by comparison on a worldly level, it would be like you, a structural engineer to design a flaw into the plane structure.

It would not be a fail-safe design. It would be a fail, unsafe design. Does that make any sense?" I asked.

"Sort of," he answered, *"I certainly wouldn't design a built in flaw,"* he agreed.

"Right! So if you, as an engineer, would not design a built in flaw, how much more would the Creator not do so either?"

"Let's use more examples: If you knew that you had a gene that would potentially pass on, and cause MS or down syndrome in an offspring, would you, as a carrier, choose to father a child?"

"I'm beginning to see your logic, based on your spiritual perception," he said, in response to my question.

"Now, Dr. Clark, the other side of the spiritual perspective is, when an individual subscribes to the love and leadership of God, God's promises kick in. One of God's promises is, that he will "never leave us nor forsake us." (Hebrews 13:5). This means despite the adversity that befalls us he (God) will help us to endure them and to cope." I stopped talking allowing time for him to absorb and process the information I had provided.

"That certainly is the way it was with Clara. I never heard her ever complain, even with all her pain and suffering," he said.

"That's a very good observation, Dr. Clark. You witnessed your wife Clara getting in touch with, and drawing on her God-given inner strength. That is a remarkable characteristic of faith followers," I told him.

"How do you get faith?" he asked.

"It is difficult to define, and even more difficult to explain, but the way to say what faith is, is believing in something that is intangible. Something you can't see, smell, or touch," I said.

"Permit me to give you an example: You go to the airport, buy a ticket to a given destination, go through security, and board the plane. You put your faith and trust in the pilot and co-pilot, but you have never met them, you don't know their names, and, in fact, you don't even know whether they are good, bad or fair pilots. As a matter of fact, you don't even personally know that they can fly the plane you are seated on.

Yet, you put your faith and trust in their hands to get you to your destination. That is faith," I said, explaining my example, and asking, *"Dr. Clark, does any of these examples make any sense to you?"*

"The examples and illustrations about faith do, but I'm not sure about faith in religion," he said.

I replied, *"I appreciate your honesty. I could go on talking about faith and trust for hours, but it would probably not be any clearer to you. For the person who is seeking to learn faith, there comes a point where you just have to believe, to receive faith,"* I answered.

"What does that mean?" he asked.

"You have to make up your mind that you are going to believe in. That is, believe in yourself; your ability to achieve or belief in a higher power. Once you want to believe in, or to accept something through faith, for example, that there is a Higher Power, you began asking that Higher Power for increased faith," I said.

"It sounds complicated," he answered.

"I know it sounds complex, but it is really very simple," I told him.

"Explain the simplicity to me," he invited.

I attempted to explain the simple dynamics of spirituality; belief in a Higher Power; acceptance of that Higher Power as a spiritual reality; communication with that Higher Power for greater understanding, and for guidance in learning a deep faith."

"Is this an understandable explanation, Dr. Clark?" I asked.

"It's starting to make sense. I am beginning to understand what my wife Clara was trying to teach me for so many years," he answered, and continued, *"Bless her heart, I just wouldn't listen; now it's too late,"* he sadly said.

"It's never too late to learn faith, Dr. Clark," I said. *"Life is fragile short and short, we need to learn to handle it with care."*

Abruptly, he changed the subject and said, *"What about me? I'm 83 years old and the doctor said I have cardiomyopathy. That's not surprising. I've had a heart condition for years. He said "My diagnosis is very terminal; I could die at any time."*

"How did that make you feel?" I asked.

"Sad, at first, but after all, I am an old man, and I have lived a very full life, and that's O.K. I don't really have anything to live for, since Clara is gone," he told me.

"Have I answered all your questions satisfactorily?" I asked.

"Yes. You've given me a lot to think about. I'll take all that you said into consideration," he answered.

"Good. I will be seeing you again with your permission. If you have any other questions, or just want to talk, please call me," I invited.

"I will, Chaplain; I will," he responded, and then said, *"Just one more question. Based on my diagnosis, my condition, and your experience, how long do you think I have to live?"* he asked.

I thought for a few seconds and then replied.

"Dr. Clark, you have voiced your skepticism about knowing whether there is a God by saying, 'If there is a God.'"

"Permit me to answer your question by re-stating your belief. 'If there is a God,' only that same God knows.

Dr. Clark said, *"Touché,"* and shook my hand. *"Chaplain, you are an interesting religious person; I like you. Please come again, soon,"* he invited.

He held open the door for me as I exited the home and walked toward the elevator.

Unfortunately, Dr. Clark's invitation went unaccepted. The following week I learned, that he had sustained a massive heart attack, and died an instantaneous death.

CHAPTER 50

It Would Help Pay the Airfare

Alberta Stewart, an 83 year old Caucasian female had been diagnosed with end-stage congestive heart failure (CHF), a terminal illness. Her doctor had referred her to the hospice agency where I serve as Chaplain.

During the start of care evaluation for hospice she had requested to see a Chaplain, as soon as possible.

I was assigned to her case and I called to schedule an appointment.

"Mrs. Stewart, this is Curtis, the hospice Chaplain. I'm calling to schedule an appointment with you which you asked for," I said.

"Oh, yes, Chaplain. Thank you for calling. When would you like to see me?" she asked.

"At your convenience; name a day and a time," I answered.

"What about tomorrow, Chaplain?" she asked her.

"Good. What time?" I asked.

"I sleep late, make it after 2 PM," she replied.

"How about 3 PM; will that be all right?" I asked to confirm the appointment time.

"That'll do just fine," she said.

I arrived at the home and was let in by a granddaughter, and two poodles who appeared to be ferociously barking. The granddaughter yelled at the dogs: *"Cinnamon! Ginger! Be quiet!"* and then turned to me and said, *"They won't bite, they just make a lot of noise,"* she tried to assure me.

I was not so convinced that they wouldn't bite, and asked, *"Are you sure?"*

"They never have," she said, again trying to assure me.

I heard a voice, from what appeared to be the back area of the house, *"Carla, put those dogs in the bedroom!"*

"O.K., Gramma, I will," granddaughter Carla replied, came in, scooped up the dogs in her arms and headed for the bedroom.

I walked toward the voice and observed a heavy-set woman sitting at the table of what appeared to be a kitchenette/dining room combination. She was wearing a floral MuMu and continuously using oxygen.

"Come on in, Chaplain. Pardon me for not getting up. I'm Alberta; call me Berta," she said.

I made my way across the floor side-stepping magazines, newspapers, a Geometry book, and house slippers.

"Sorry for the mess, my granddaughters are not very neat and tidy," she apologized.

"No problem," I said, *"It doesn't bother me at all."*

She extended her hand in greeting, shook my hand, and then said, *"Have a seat."*

"I'm Chaplain Curtis, I spoke to you by phone," I said.

"Yes. Thank you for coming. I wanted to see you; I have some questions," she said.

"I'll be pleased to answer any questions I feel comfortable with," I told her.

"Good. First, let me give you a little family history background. As you can probably see, me, my daughter Colleen, and granddaughters Carla and Connie all live here. It's not always easy with my poor health. I was living in Arizona alone and my health started failing. I figured it would be better to move in with them, rather than try to go to a board and care home. Especially since Colleen is a single parent. I wanted to share their expenses, and, at the same time, help

them out, financially. I'm not wealthy, but I have some savings. So here I am," she said, and stopped talking.

She went on to say, *"I don't know how much longer I have to live. My doctor doesn't give me much hope, because my heart is failing fast. I can hardly breathe, even with oxygen."*

"What did the doctor tell you, Berta?" I asked.

"He told me heart condition is very serious, especially because of my weight. But at age 83 there's not much I can do about that. I love to eat, and my appetite is still good. I guess I'm only going to live 'til I die anyway, Chaplain," she said, trying to lighten the subject.

I smiled at her humor and said, *"One can't argue with that,"* and then asked, *"How can I be of help?"*

"Chaplain, first of all, I want to know where I stand with the Lord," she said.

"What does that mean?" I asked, for clarification in knowing where she was going with the conversation.

"Well, I want to know that my soul is secure when I die," she answered. *What is your belief system, and do you have a particular denomination?"* I asked, trying not to sound like an interrogator.

"I'm a Protestant. I was raised in a non-denominational church, the Church of God," she said, and continued, *"But I haven't been to church in years. So I just want to be sure of my relationship to God."*

"Would you want me to contact a Church of God minister to come and talk with you?" I asked.

"I was told you were a Protestant minister. You will do," she answered.

"Yes, I am. If you feel comfortable with me, I will be pleased to be your pastor," I told her.

"I'd like that," she replied.

"O.K., if you're sure," I said.

"I'm sure," she said, confirming her answer.

We talked about her religious experience as a child. She said, *"I followed the teaching of my church, had a spiritual* *awakening, and invited Christ into my heart as personal Savior."* Were you baptized?"* I asked.

"Yes. I was baptized when I was 14," she replied.

"Sometimes when a person has not been active in their church for a long time, and they are feeling unsure of their relationship with God, I often suggest to them that, they might want to re-new their vows of faith in God, and to re-dedicate their lives to the Lord. Does that sound like something that you would like to do?" I asked.

"Oh, yes, Chaplain, I want to do that," she answered.

I was pleased to be able to pray with her and lead her in a prayer re-dedicating her life to Christ, and re-newing her vows of faith in Christ as her personal Savior; I prayed God would grant unto her the desires of her heart and give her a great sense of peace.

Berta, as she wanted to be called, appeared to be getting tired, and was struggling with breathing.

"I'm going to be leaving now, Berta. May I come see you again?" I asked.

"Oh, yes, please do," she said. She stood up to give me a hug, and kissed me on the cheek. *"I'll see you, when I see you; I always call ahead"* I told her, shook her hand, and let myself out.

In on-going visits Berta became 'very fond of you (me)' (her words). With each visit she shared more and more of her life in review.

On one of the visits, the subject of vacation comes up. She asked where I planned to go on my vacation.

"My wife and I plan to go to Hawaii this year, for a much needed rest" I told her.

She asked about our finances. She said, *"Without being nosy, will you have enough money to have a great vacation?"*

"Yes," I assured her, *"Finances will not be a problem."*

"The reason I ask, Chaplain, is because you are going to conduct my funeral memorial Service, (she had previously asked if I would officiate her memorial service and I had agreed to do so), and I'm going to pay you for it. So I thought, if you needed some money to help

out with your vacation, I would be glad to give you the money now in advance. It would help pay the airfare," she generously offered.

"That is very kind of you, Berta, but I wouldn't be able to accept your money now, or later. It would be inappropriate and a conflict of interest. However, you could give the money to a non-profit, faith-based organization like the National Heart or National Cancer Society," I told her.

With tears in her eyes she said, "Chaplain, I want you to know, you have become an important part of my life and family. I will never forget your unselfish help."

Berta's condition exacerbated and she changed remarkably. During the week I was away on vacation she had become bed bound, with decreased energy and decreased strength.

I received an urgent message to call her daughter at their home. I placed the call and spoke with Colleen.

"Chaplain, the nurse told us that mother is actively dying. She is asking for you," she said..."

"I will be there as soon as possible," I told her and walked toward my car.

Upon arriving at the home I was shown into Berta's bed room. The RN Case Manager, the daughter Connie, and two granddaughters Carla and Connie were gathered around her bed.

Berta's eyes were closed when I moved to her bedside and held her hand. I spoke into her ear and she opened her eyes, and then closed them I sensed a faint movement of her lips suggesting a smile. I asked her to squeeze my hand if she could hear me. I continued to hold her hand I turned and spoke to the family and spoke to them

"I'm going to say some prayers for Berta, and then I want us to hold hands as we recite the Our Father prayer, after which, I will anoint her with oil and give her a blessing."

After facilitating the prayers, the anointing and the blessing for Alberta, I then asked a blessing upon the family"

"May the Lord bless you and keep you, The Lord make his face *shine upon you, and be gracious unto you; The Lord lift up his countenance upon you, and give you peace," (Numbers 6:24).*

I asked the daughter Connie to call me if needed, and walked out of the bed room.

The next morning I received a call telling me that Berta had passed that evening at 5:25 PM.

I called Connie to express my condolence and tried to share with her some words of comfort. *"Connie, your mother was well prepared spiritually, to go home to be with the Lord. The Scriptures tell us that, 'To be absent from the body, is to be present with the Lord,'"(II Corinthians 5:8)."*

And today, consistent with her Christian belief system, Alberta's spirit is with God; in that Heavenly home not made with hands, called Paradise.

CHAPTER 51

A Hospice Chaplains' Reflection

As a hospice chaplain, working with terminally ill patients, it is always a blessing to be able to discuss with them their belief system, and to explore their relationship to a Higher Power.

I am reminded of one particular patient who had contracted stomach cancer. Joe Wellington greeted me with an infectious smile. Soft-spoken and appearing to be easy-going, his buoyant attitude defied his life-threatening illness. His demeanor caused me to like him at once, and we seemed to *"connect,"* gaining immediate rapport.

As we talked, he shared with me _ in life review _ some of his experiences. He was a WWII United States Marine Veteran, and a Pearl Harbor survivor. He had just recently been diagnosed with cancer, and the oncologist confirmed his life expectancy as being three to six months or less.

I asked what his belief system was. He said, *"Protestant, I guess,"* and continued. *"I went to a Methodist when I was a kid.."* Further discussion revealed that he did not presently have a connection with a local church, and had not attended in years. Joe was anxious to talk about his relationship with a Higher power; he wondered if he *had* one.

I encouraged him to openly talk about his experience as a child at Sunday school, and Church. At first he seemed a little uncomfortable but continued talking.

"I really don't remember too much about it, I guess it didn't hold my interest." he said.

I asked if he would like for me to explain what his church taught about a 'personal relationship to God?' He gave me permission and indicated that he was eager to listen. I shared with him the teachings and disciplines of the Methodist church with regard to their theology, i.e., 'a personal relationship with God through the acceptance of Christ _ by invitation _ into the believer's heart.'

I concluded the explanation by asking if he had followed the teachings of *his* churches doctrine.

"No," he replied, *"I guess I never did."*

I then asked, if he would like for me, *"To facilitate a Methodist minister to his home, who could help him in making such a decision?"*

"No," he said. *"You are a Chaplain, aren't you a minister? Can't you help me make the decision"* he asked.

"Yes. I am a minister," I told him, *"And yes, I can pray with you, and help you make a decision for Christ.*

I was privileged to pray with him, and assist him, with a reconciliation of faith decision which _ according to the teachings of his own belief system, and the Methodist church _ assured him of eternal life for his soul, after physical death.

Joe Wellington _ U.S. Marine Corps WWII Veteran, and Pearl Harbor survivor _ showed no embarrassment, and offered no apology for the tears filling his eyes and sliding down his cheeks; neither did he have to.

Seemingly at peace with himself _ and God, as he *now* knew him _ Joe thanked me, shook my hand, and invited me to *"Come back again, Chaplain, anytime."*

CHAPTER 52

Walking Through the Valley

This is a true story of the devastating effects of tobacco, by Diane Modglin, as told to Chaplain Curtis E. Smith, Ph.D., who was, at the time, Senior Staff Chaplain at Brea Community Hospital, Brea, California.

"My name is Diane Modglin. I was born October 5, 1932, in Long Beach, California, to Roberta and Albert Grant. Both were heavy smokers. Since I was an only child, I don't remember ever wanting for anything. I had loving parents who were very good to me. I idolized them, and looked up to them as role models.

"Although my parents didn't insist, I worked at odd jobs during summer break and after school during my high school years. Deciding not to go to college right after I graduated, I took a job in a supermarket. I soon discovered that I was surrounded by many persons who smoked. I was, according to the, the only "square." The peer pressure was overwhelming. I gave in and started smoking when I was 20.

Although both of my parents smoked, they tried to tell me that smoking was a bad habit and could harm my health. My dad said he had emphysema from smoking. I still didn't listen. My grandmother cried when she first saw me smoking. Until the day she died she tried to get me to quit.

She would say, "Diane, when you abuse your body, you're going to kill yourself." Again, I didn't listen.

While working at the supermarket, I met a young man who stole my heart. I fell madly in love and married Ray Randall when I was 21. One year later, I gave birth to my oldest child, Carrie. At about this same time my marriage started to fall apart. I didn't understand why until years later.

"Ray was a devout follower of his faith and religion. Having been reared in mainstream Fundamental Christendom, I didn't agree with his church's teachings. The difference was the cause for our many disagreements; we ultimately separated and divorced after only four years of marriage.

"I then met Jerry. Four years later we were married. We were perfectly matched. It seemed as though our marriage was not only blessed in heaven but made there. We had been married three years when I got pregnant with our second daughter, Tawnya.

"Time passed. I started going to church again. Although I had been in and out of church all my life, I never became a Christian until I started studying the Bible. I was blessed abundantly. I had a wonderful family, a loving husband, and a happy marriage.

I Felt Guilty. "*Active in church again, I spent hours reading the Bible and eventually started feeling guilty about smoking, yet I didn't stop; this made me feel even more guilty. I came across a pamphlet written to encourage people to quit smoking. It said, If others can stop smoking YOU can!*

If others can quit, YOU can TOO!" I felt even more guilty. I finally quit.

"I stopped smoking for three years, but I was not prepared for the struggle I would go through. During a low time in my life I fell away from the church. Jerry was away from home often.

The long evenings and loneliness progressed. Every magazine and newspaper screamed at me with advertisements about low-tar cigarettes that were new on the market. "Low- tar and nicotine cigarettes with filters that greatly reduce the harmful effects of smoking.'

"With that stamp of approval I was hooked again. Just a few cigarettes in the evening at first, then before I realized it I was back to one pack, then two packs a day.

"As I look back, it wasn't the lonely nights, or Jerry being away, or even the cigarette advertising that had been responsible for my starting to smoke again. I had used those reasons as "crutches." My crazed desire for nicotine had won out. My value judgment was faulty. I was the one to blame.

My Body Changed. "I started feeling physical changes in my body. I began to have great difficulty breathing and my energy was very low. I couched uncontrollable at night.

About this time my daughter Tawnya was having her twenty-sixth birthday. As I did for every family birthday, I prepared for a party that would include dozens of balloons that I would have to blow up by mouth. But this time, however, I discovered I couldn't blow up even one balloon. I didn't think too much about these changes. I didn't consider it a health condition. I excused my inability to blow up the balloons by blaming the balloons for being smaller and stronger. My difficulty breathing and low energy level are just because I'm getting older, I thought. I didn't believe anything was wrong with me _except the cough. It persisted and worsened. My husband insisted that I go to the doctor. I reluctantly made and kept an appointment.

"At the doctor's office I was given a breath test with a spirogram. I was to blow into an apparatus that measured my lung's ability to inhale and exhale. I could not exhale and blow hard enough to get the dial to register. It stayed at zero. I flunked the test. A chest X-ray was distorted.

"They could not make a positive diagnosis. The doctors continued to test me, but could not determine what was wrong. I was scheduled for exploratory surgery. An inoperable tumor mass was discovered in my chest behind my left breast." "How Could This Happen to Me?

"When I heard the news I was devastated. How could this be

happening to me? I'm only 58 years old. I knew I shouldn't blame God for something I had caused, but I did.

"I was listening, but didn't want to hear what three oncology specialists were telling me; that I should take chemotherapy because I had a 70 percent chance for the tumor mass to be reduced and go into remission.

"I was in shock. I had cancer; I was going to die! When I said that to the chief oncology doctor he replied, "So am I. We all are going to die. Some of us are just going to die sooner that others."

He went on to explain that the difference with cancer patients is not that they are "dying with cancer" _ (rather) they are "living with cancer."

"Initially I struggled with the decision of whether or not to take chemotherapy. I had always heard how sick you get and how helpless and hopeless you feel with nausea, vomiting, diarrhea, and eventual hair loss. I didn't want to lose my hair. This may sound ridiculous, but running my fingers through my long strands, I suddenly realized just how much my hair was a part of me. I imagined that when it started to fall out, it would be like watching my body disintegrate before my own eyes.

"Should I take a treatment that will put me completely out of control? Should I let my desire for control and dignity stand in the way of possible remission? I finally made the decision _ I would take the first chemotherapy treatment."

"Everything I had heard about the side effects of chemotherapy was true. I was never so sick in my life! I vowed I would never take another treatment! It wasn't worth it just to stay alive. God, just let me die now!

"Through the efforts and prayers of oncologists, the hospital chaplain, and the support of my family, I was persuaded to go through a battery of chemotherapy treatments.

"At the time of this writing I am getting a treatment every two weeks. I have a better than average chance for remission and an opportunity for several years of extended life. I am praying for a

miracle. I already know that I have been abundantly blessed. I have become acquainted with the 'valley of the shadow of death' spoken of by the psalmist. I have not experienced any more severe side effects from the chemotherapy. I still have most of my hair, but I know that won't last. I am prepared to become bald.

"As I look back over my relatively short life, I am angry. Not at God, but angry because at 58 years of age my life is wasted. My body is racked with pain. At best my future is too short. Because I abused the gift of life, I am dying. I suffer. My family suffers with me and for me. When I die they will mourn my death."

"I finally now know what my grandmother was trying to tell me _ *'When you abuse your body, you're going to kill yourself.'* I have stopped smoking. Why did I quit? What did I have to gain? I'm going to die anyway. I quit because I have discovered a love beyond myself.

One that has drawn me into a closer relationship with my dear ones _ my family, and God. A caring love that compels me to reach out and share my story.

"I tell about this experience so that others who are hooked on nicotine _ like I was _ may know that whatever pleasure you may get of smoking, is not worth the risk of developing cancer and dying!

"I quit smoking the day I visited the doctor's office and discovered I had a spot on my lungs that was cancer. For me that was too late. For you, it doesn't have to be.

WRITER'S NOTE: Diane died on December 22, 1990, from lung cancer caused by smoking cigarettes. This maker her message even more emphatic for you __ the reader __ stop smoking, before it is too late.

AUTHOR'S NOTE: This true story first appeared in the Adventist Review in 1990, a publication of the Review and Herald Publishing Association, Hagertown, MD. It is used here with permission of the author and publisher.

CHAPTER 53

An Honored Request

At the request of one of my church members, who was diagnosed with breast cancer, and who asked that her story be included, even though she is not a Hospice Patient, this Post Script has been added.

As beneficial and valuable as the Hospice program of palliative care treatment, for freedom from pain, and patient comfort is, there are still some who elect to maintain a medical modality of aggressive treatment as an alternative. Mary Boorenanpang (her real name with her permission) is such a person.

Approximately one year ago, she was diagnosed with a terminal illness, and opted early on to, pursue aggressive treatment through chemotherapy. At the time of this writing, she had undergone 15 chemotherapy treatments and continues to receive chemotherapy treatments three times a week, Monday, Wednesday, and Friday.

The chemo treatments drives the white blood cell count up, and, to offset the high white count, Mary receives injections to increase her red blood cell count, on alternate days of the week, Tuesdays and Thursdays.

Mary is a remarkable lady. A fine Christian person who, despite her loss of energy and strength, and frequent hospitalizations, continues to be a faithful, intermittent, church attendee, depending on her physical condition permitting.

Shortly after the onset of her life limiting illness she lost 15 pounds in two months. She also lost her raven black hair. She is able to meticulously compensate for the loss of her hair by cosmetically wearing a lovely hair piece made from human hair.

When Mary is unable to attend church, the church is able to take "church" to Mary, via the Pastor and his wife Sandra.

At the time of this writing Mary continues to receive chemotherapy treatments, and she is receiving blood transfusion dependent ever 3 to 4 weeks.

On a recent visit with Mary, she related to me, as her pastor, that from a spiritual perspective, she had undergone a remarkable attitude change.

Whereas, after the onset of her life limiting illness, she worried constantly about her husband, adult children, and grandchildren, as to what would happen to them upon her demise.

After approximately a year of on-going curative, aggressive medical treatment she shared with me that her attitude *had* changed.

No longer does she worry about 'after she is gone;' her family's finances, status, or well- being. Rather, she says, she has *"completely turned her life, her family, and her physical condition over to God, with the full knowledge that, when she is gone, she will be in Heaven, where she will again one day, be with her family, and everything will be O.K."*

AUTHOR'S NOTE: Mary lost her long battle with cancer and passed from this life on May 21, 2009 having reached the age of 62 years.

POSTLUDE:

A Backward and Forward Look

In preparing for publication of the Second Edition of this work titled *"Walking Through The Valley"* (published under the title of *"When It's Time,"* in the First Edition), the author took opportunity to review and re-read, *often with tear-filled eyes*, many of the true stories contained herein. The content continues to amaze and inspire.

Dr. Curtis remains active in the Hospice industry ministering to the Hospice patients' point of spiritual need.

It is a blessing and privilege to be able to connect with people at their point of need specifically as they enter the end-of-life's journey and they start thinking about where their Spirit will spend eternity and their personal relationship to a Higher Power.

While the Second Edition contains much of previously published material, the work has been expanded to include the following:

Postlude: A Backward and Forward Look Caring For the Caregiver; Tips for Being Good to Yourself Tips for Stress Reduction An Article For Encouragement: Think About This Affirmations Terminal Diseases Glossary: Basic Diagnoses Definitions Hospice Philosophy The Hospice Chaplain About the Author

Each of these additional sections is presented for emotional and life-enhancement application by the family member caregiver, professional paid caregiver, clinician and medical practiner.

DISCLAIMER

The suggestions presented, is material widely used by psychotherapists and Professional Counselors _ with caregivers who work in the health care profession _ when conferencing for anxiety, depression, and stress reduction.

Subsequently, there is no intent to plaragize any of these terms and/or suggestions; they are easily recognized, and widely used, by counseling professionals in the health care industry.

When material is used where the source is known, it has been properly credited.

Caregiving is a very demanding and intense task when caring for patients; it is especially stressful for caregivers who work with terminally ill patients at the end of life's journey.

Therefore, it is a foregone conclusion, and extremely necessary, for caregivers to learn and practice suggested methods for reduction of stress, anxiety, and depression in order to avoid "caregiver burnout."

It is with that thought in mind that these broadly used terms and suggestions are provided to aid and assist both family members, and professional caregivers, a "need-to-know" pathway to stress reduction techniques, enabling them to "*connect*" with information on *how,* to *care* for the caregiver.

CARING FOR THE CAREGIVER; TIPS FOR BEING GOOD TO YOURSELF

Take "time" for you; be "good" to yourself.

Be a responsible person to others; don't sacrifice yourself for other's sake.

Stay away from negative people and situations that stress you. Get closer to positive people and situations that energize you.

Learn more about the art of taking. Allow people to do things for you.

You can become a "self-caregiver." Concentrate on things that remind you of love and, "who" you are.

Don't let feelings of "guilt" overcome you for some short-coming; stay positive.

Enjoy a "belly-laugh;" laughing tickles the endorphins, getting in touch with endorphins are healthy for your body and create happiness for you.

Schedule some "fun" and entertainment into your life; read a humorous book; go to a comedy movie with a friend; net-work with a friend on the telephone; go for walk or schedule a lunch with a friend.

Compliment and appreciate yourself; say good things about yourself.

Don't try to be a perfectionist; allow yourself to make a mistake once in a while, and

Forgive yourself for failure.

Be thankful for what you have; don't envy others. When you envy it means you want what they have; decide what you want and put energy into obtaining it.

The bottom line: taking care of (you) the caregiver is not selfish. Rather, it allows you to give the greatest gift; the gift of self.

TIPS FOR STRESS
REDUCTION TECHNIQUES

Eat a balanced diet; three elements are necessary to obtain, and maintain a healthy life. They are: a proper balanced diet; proper rest (7 to 8 Hours per Night), and exercise a minimum of three times per week.

STOP Smoking; REDUCE coffee, tea, caffeine, and carbonated drinks.

Drink 6 to 8 glasses of water per day: At Breakfast; Mid-morning, and Evening

Learn how to say "NO!"

Net-work with others whom you trust.

Develop a Hobby; do something you like outside of work.

Take time for refreshment and entertainment, i.e. read a book; watch TV programs that uplift your spirit; network with other by telephone, texting, or Email.

Provide for you a quiet time for relaxation, reflection and meditation.

Learn to laugh; don't take yourself too seriously.

Recognize your boundaries; use the Serenity Prayer as a Guide: "God grant me the serenity to accept the things I cannot change, the courage to change the things I can, and the wisdom to know the difference."

Make a conscious effort to visualize yourself as the person you want to be.

Be thankful to God, and others.

Claim your short-comings; take steps to change what you can, use failures as stepping stones to successful achievement.

Go for a walk; still one of the "best" exercises.

Know your priorities; set goals for achievement: short term goal; a mid-range goal, and a long-term goal; diligently work toward obtaining.

Express or "vent" your anger and frustration with someone you trust; redirect your anger or frustration through exercise.

Develop a routine for regularity in your life; Set times for Meditation; Meals; Recreation, and Spiritual practices.

Become an "Active Listener;" listen quietly for people to finish their sentences.

Arrange to have variety in your life with people, places, thoughts and things.

Frequently "reach outside the box;" stay in touch with acquaintances, friends, and family.

Laugh often; give yourself permission to laugh at yourself.

Affirm yourself and others, whom you come into contact with.

Make a doable and realistic schedule of tasks you want to accomplish each day; do not overload the schedule.

When ambulating, walk, don't run or hurry; hurrying increases stress.

When driving, drive safely, don't speed; STOP when an amber caution light flashes, don't speed through.

Don't talk on a cell phone while driving.

Don't "Text" and drive.

Take a short "Get Away" vacation. Frequent "short" vacations are better than long ones.

Think "Good Thoughts" about people you meet.

Always allow time for the "unexpected," to happen.

Always follow the "Golden Rule," i.e. "Do unto others, as you would have others do unto you."

Matthew 7:12 (Paraphrase).

AN ARTICLE FOR ENCOURAGEMENT

THINK ABOUT THIS

To laugh is appearing a fool.

To weep is to risk appearing sentimental.

To reach out for another is to risk involvement.

To expose feelings is to risk exposing your true self.

To place your ideas, your dreams, before the crowd

Is to risk their loss.

To love is to risk not being loved in return.

To live is to risk dying.

To hope is to risk despair.

To try is to risk failure.

But risks must be taken because the Greatest hazard in life

Is to risk nothing.

The person who risks nothing, does nothing, has nothing,

Is nothing.

He may avoid suffering and sorrow, but he simply cannot learn, feel,

Change, grow, love, and live,

Chained by his certitudes, he is a slave;

He has forfeited freedom.

Only a person who risks is free.

Anonymous

AFFIRMATIONS

GIFTS

In lieu of gifts
Your support for the America Cancer Society
Or your choice of a Non-Profit Corporation
Doing research in the prevention
And cure of terminal diseases
Will be appreciated.

Please make donations in the name of:
(Loved ones' name) directly to the American Cancer Society
Local City (or your choice of a Non-Profit Corporation
Doing research in the prevention
And cure of terminal diseases).
Designate that the monies be used
For continued research in the prevention
And cure of terminal illnesses.

AN AFFIRMATION
HE SET ME FREE

Don't grieve for me, for now I'm free.

I'm following the path God laid for me.

I took His hand when I heard His call,

I turned my back, and left it all.

I could not stay another day, to laugh,

To love, to work, or play.

Tasks left undone must stay that way,

I found that place at the close of day.

If my parting has left a void, then fill it

With remembered joy. A friendship shared,

A laugh, a kiss. Yes, these things I too, will miss.

Be not burdened with times of sorrow,

I wish for you the sunshine of tomorrow.

My life's been full, I savored much,

Good friends, good times, good times,

A loved one's touch.

Perhaps my time seemed all too brief,

Don't lengthen it now with undue grief,

Lift up your heart and share with me.

God wanted me now.

He set me free.

AN AFFIRMATION
STRENGTH ANEW

It's difficult when someone
Who is loved cannot be there,
But memories that are made and shared,
Will keep a loved one near.
And God, with loving wisdom,
Will be there to guide us through;
He'll help us meet tomorrow
And He'll give us strength anew.

AN AFFIRMATION
LOVE AND GO ON

You can shed tears that (she / he) is gone,

Or you can smile because (she / he) has lived.

You can shed tears that (she / he) is gone,

Or you can smile because (she / he) has lived.

Or can close your eyes and pray that (she / he)

Will come back, or you can open your eyes

And see all that (she's / he's) left.

Our heart can be empty because you can't see

(Her / him), or you can be full of the love you shared.

You can turn your back on tomorrow

And live yesterday, or you can be happy for

Tomorrow because of yesterday.

You can remember (her / him) and only that she's

He's) gone, or you can cherish (her / his) memory

And let it live on.

You can cry and close your mind, be empty and

Turn your back, or you can do what (she / he) wants:

Smile, open your eyes, love and go on.

AN AFFIRMATION

FLY

Fly, fly little wing; Fly beyond imagining. The softest
Cloud, the whitest doves, Upon the wind of Heaven's love.
Past the planets and the stars, Leave this lonely world of ours.
Escape the sorrow and the pain. And fly again.
Fly, fly precious one. Your endless journey has just begun.
Take your gentle happiness, far too beautiful for this.
Cross over to the shore. There is peace forevermore.
But hold this memory bittersweet, until we meet again.

AN AFFIRMATION

THANK YOU

Perhaps you sent a lovely card,

Or sat quietly in a chair;

Perhaps you sent beautiful flowers,

If so, we saw them thee.

Perhaps you sent or spoke kind words

As any friend would say;

Perhaps you were not there at all

Just thought of us *that* day.

Whatever you did to console the heart,

We thank you so much, for whatever the part.

AN AFFIRMATION
MEMORIES LIVE FOREVER

Memories live forever,

They grow richer through the years.

They are nurtured by our laughter,

They are watered by our tears.

Memories live forever,

Sent from Heaven above.

To eternally connect us

To the people we so dearly love.

Thank you for your prayers.

Love and kind expressions of sympathy.

God Bless You!

The Family

AN AFFIRMATION
PRAYER OF ST. FRANCIS OF ASSISI

Lord make me an instrument of Thy Peace

Where there is hatred, let me show love.

Where there is injury, pardon.

Where there is doubt, faith.

Where there is despair, hope.

Where there is darkness, light.

Where there is sadness, joy.

O Divine Master,

Grant that I may not so much seek

To be consoled as to console;

To be understood as to understand,

To be loved as to love;

For it is in giving that we receive,

It is in pardoning that we are pardoned,

And it is in dying that we are born to

Eternal life.

AN AFFIRMATION
LEGACY OF LOVE

A wife, (husband) a mother, (father), my granny too,

This is the legacy we have for you,

You taught us love and how to fight,

You gave us strength, you gave us might.

A stronger person would be hard to find,

And in your heart, you were always kind.

You fought for us ALL in one way or another,

Not just as a granny, wife or mother.

For ALL of us, you gave your best,

Now the time has come for you to rest.

So go in peace, you've earned your sleep,

Your love in our hearts, we'll eternally keep.

AN AFFIRMATION
ACKNOWLEDGEMENT OF APPRECIATION

The family wishes to acknowledge

With deep appreciation the many

Comforting messages, floral tributes,

Prayers and every other expression of

Kindness and concern during this time.

AN AFFIRMATION
SERENITY PRAYER

God grant me the Serenity

To accept the things I cannot change

The Courage to change the things I can

And the Wisdom to know the difference.

Amen

AN AFFIRMATION
IN OUR HEART FOREVER

You left us without saying goodbye

Now we must let go with a heavy sigh.

There are no words to express the pain

Just Precious memories that remain.

Drifting thoughts of what may have been said

Or maybe, just to hold you a while instead.

So many things to miss about you

Your stories, laughter and faces you do.

Great talks beginning with "You'll never believe this,"

Thinking ahead to the conversations we'll miss.

Wanting to push this day off till never

But know you will stay in our hearts forever.

AN AFFIRMATION
THE 23RD. PSALM

The Lord is my shepherd;

I shall not want. He causes me to

lie down in green pastures, He leads me

Beside the still water He restores my soul.

He leads me in the Paths of righteousness

For His name's sake. Yea, though I walk

Through the valley of the Shadow of death, You

Are with me; your rod and your staff they comfort

Me; You prepare a table before me in the presence

Of my enemies: You anoint my head with oil;

My cup runs over, surely goodness and mercy

Will follow me all the days of my life: and I will

Dwell in the house of the Lord forever. 23rd. Psalm KJV

AN AFFIRMATION
A NEW COMMANDMENT

"A new commandment I give to you,
That you love one another." ___ John 13:34
Offered in the belief that a heart filled with
Love knows no separation from those who
Live on in memory.

AN AFFIRMATION
APPRECIATION

On behalf of the family
We express our gratitude for your
Many kindnesses evidenced in
Thought and deeds over the years,
And your attendance at this
Memorial Service.

AN AFFIRMATION
THE BEYOND

It seemed such a little way to me,

Across to that strange country, The Beyond;

And yet, not strange, for it has grown to be

The home, for those of whom I am so fond.

And so for me there is no death;

It is but crossing with abated breath,

A little strip of sea,

To find one's loved ones waiting on the

Shore, more beautiful, more precious than before.

Ella Wheel Wilcox

AN AFFIRMATION

GONE BUT NOT FORGOTTEN

A precious one from us has gone

A voice we love is stilled;

A place is vacant in our home,

This never can be filled.

The boon their love has given,

And though the body slumbers here,

The soul is safe in Heaven.

AN AFFIRMATION
I DO NOT SLEEP

Do not stand at my grave and weep;

I am not there. I do not sleep;

I am a thousand winds that blow,

I am the diamond glint on snow.

I am the sunlight on ripened grain,

I am the gentle autumn rain.

When you awake in the morning's hush,

I am the swift uplifting rush

Of quiet birds in circling flight.

I am the soft star shine at night.

Do not stand at my grave and cry;

I am not there. I did not die.

AN AFFIRMATION
REMEMBER ME

Fill not your hearts with pain and sorrow

But remember me in every tomorrow,

Remember the joy, the laughter, the smiles,

I've only gone to rest for a while.

Although my leaving causes pain and grief,

My going has eased my hurt

And given me relief.

So dry your eyes and remember me,

Not as I am now, but as I used to be.

Because, I will remember you all

And look on with a smile.

Understand in your hearts,

I've only gone to rest a little while.

As long as I have the love of each of you,

I can live my life

In the hearts of all of you.

AN AFFIRMATION
A LIGHT IS GONE

A light is from our household gone,
A voice we loved is stilled.
A place is vacant in our home
This never can be filled.
We have to mourn the loss of one
We did our best to save.
Beloved on earth, regretted still,
Remembered in the grave.
'Twas hard to part with one so dear,
We little thought the time was near
Farewell, dear one, your life is past,
Our love for you till the end will last.

AN AFFIRMATION
AMERICAN INDIAN POEM

When I am dead

Cry for me a little

Think of me sometimes

But not too much.

It is not good for you

Or your wife or your husband

Or your children

To allow your thoughts to dwell

Too long on the dead.

Think of me now and again

As I was in life

At some moment it is pleasant to recall.

But not for long.

Leave me in peace,

And I shall leave you, too, in peace.

While you live:

Let your thoughts be with the living.

AN AFFIRMATION

BIRDS OF SORROW

You cannot prevent the birds of sorrow

From flying over your head,

But you can prevent them from

building a nest in your hair.

CHINESE PROVERB

AN AFFIRMATION

ONLY THE BEST

God saw that _____

Name of deceased

Was getting tired, and life was no longer to be

So He put his arms around _____

Her / Him

And whispered, _____ come home with me.

Name of deceased

With tearful eyes we watched _____

Her / Him

And prayed for _____ each day,

Her / Him

Although we loved _____ dearly,

Her / Him

We could not ask _____ to stay.

Her / Him

A golden heart stopped beating; hardworking hands came to rest.
God broke our hearts, to prove to us, He only takes the best.

AN AFFIRMATION
TWO SMILING EYES

Two smiling eyes are sleeping,
Two busy hands are still;
The one we love so deeply
Is resting at God's will.
May (she / he) always walk in sunshine
God's around (her / him) Glow.
For all the happiness (she / he) gave us,
Only a few will ever know.
It broke our hearts to lose (her / him)
But, (she / he) did not go alone.
For part of our hearts went with (her / him)
The day God called (her / him) home.

TERMINAL DISEASES

Medicare publishes guidelines which specify diseases which qualify for hospice as terminal. In order to qualify for Medicare hospice coverage the diagnosis has to be certified by two medical doctors ___ usually the patient's primary care physician, and the hospice medical director ___ that the prospective patient has one or more terminal diseases, or else qualifies under the non-specific category designated as "failure to thrive."

The most common and debilitating are metastatic cancer, which represents for more than fifty percent of all hospice patient; irreparable organ failure, such as decompensated cirrhosis of the liver; uremia (renal failure) not amenable to dialysis; Stage IV Congestive Heart Failure CHF); irreversible respiratory failure; sepsis (destruction of tissue by bacterial toxins), and anoxic encephalopathy.

Modern medicine, medical research, life support equipment, and technology can postpone the onset of death. However, advanced technology presents challenges and opportunities. Patients with a life-limiting chronic or terminal illness, in fact, often receive little or no benefit from such medical treatments; and the treatments may increase the burden of living. For instance, such treatments may only extend the symptoms of the underlying disease.

Palliative care can alleviate the symptoms exhibited by these terminal illnesses. The most common symptoms are: dyspnea (painful and labored breathing); respiratory secretions; dysphagia (difficulty in swallowing); cough; painful hiccups; nausea, vomiting; cachexia (word pronounced: ka-kecks-e-a – dehydration and emaciation); constipation; diarrhea; bowel obstruction; pruritus (skin inflammation); neuropathy (nerve pain); fatigue, anxiety; severe depression; delirium, and combinations of these symptoms.

THE MOST COMMON DISEASES	LESS COMMON QUALIFYING DISEASES
• Cancer	*Huntington's' Chorea
• Stroke	*Paralysis Agitans (Parkinson's Disease)
• Acute Cerebrovascular Accident (CVA)	*Joint Osteoporosis
• Dementia	*Intracranial Hemorrhage
• Alzheimer's Dementia	(caused by rupture of an aneurysm)
• Cardiac Disease	*Senile Degenerate Brain
• Heart Disease Congestive Heart Failure (CHF)	*Anemia
• Pulmonary Disease	
• Chronic Obstructive Pulmonary Disease (COPD)	
• Emphysema	
• Liver Disease (Cirrhosis , primary)	
• Renal Disease (Kidney Failure)	

GLOSSARY:
BASIC DIAGNOSES DEFINITIONS

*DEFINITIONS OF DIAGNOSIS AND MEDICAL TERMS:
Listed in Order of Commonality

NOTE: These Diagnostic Definitions and Terms are presented in brevity, not in the medical sense, rather in the general sense, to offer general information and insight into terminal diagnoses (many which are referred to in the text of this publication).

The Diagnostic Definitions and Terms presented herewith *are not intended to definitively identify any medical condition classified as a diagnosis.*

Any and all patients and families *are strongly urged* to conference with their own physician and/or medical practioner provider to determine a definitive diagnosis for *any health condition.*

CANCER: Cancer is an abnormal, malignant growth of cells that invade nearby tissues and often spread (*metastasize*) to other sites in the body. The majority forms of cancer can be traced to specific causative factors (e.g., cigarette smoking, overexposure to the sun); genetic (*familial*) tendencies also play a role in certain forms of cancer.

Types of Cancer: Different types of cancer vary with age, ethnic group, sex and geographic location. In the United States cancer is second only to heart disease as a cause of death; breast and lung cancer lead the statistics.

Probability of Getting: Elderly persons are more prone to cancer:

At age 25 the probability of developing cancer in 5 years is 1 in 700; at age 65, it is 1 in 14.

Most Affected Body Parts: The parts of the body most affected by cancer are the breast; lungs; colon; uterus; oral cavity, and bone marrow.

Major Signs of Cancer: The major signs and symptoms of cancer may include a change in bladder or bowel habits causing incontinence; a sore that does not heal; a persistent cough or hoarseness; unusual bleeding; a lump in the breast or other part of the body; indigestion or difficulty in swallowing; rapid and unexplained weight loss; and changes in a warts or moles.

Treatment: The treatment for cancer may involve surgery, and/or chemotherapy and radiation. The prognosis depends on the type and site of the cancer, and the promptness for obtaining initial treatment.

Probability of Cure: Approximately one-third of patients with newly diagnosed cancers are ultimately *permanently* cured.

When a Cancer Becomes Hospice Appropriate: Cancer can be diagnosed as Hospice Appropriate when the disease does not respond to the modality of curative medical treatment, and exacerbates through metastasizing (spreading) to other organs, causing the body to become weakened and to exhibit atypical signs and symptoms.
STROKE: (See Cerebrovascular accident (CVA)

CEREBROVASCULAR ACCIDENT (CVA): An abnormal condition in which hemorrhage or blockage of the blood vessels of the brain leads to oxygen starvation and symptoms, e.g., sudden loss of ability to move a body part (such as an arm, leg or the face) or to speak. Paralysis; weakness; or if severe can result in death; typically, only one side of the body is affected.

DEMENTIA: Dementia is a progressive mental decline, specifically of memory function and judgment, usually accompanied by disorientation, stupor, and radical change in the personality. When Dementia is caused by a disease, such as Alzheimer's, by brain injury, or by degenerate brain brought about through aging (senile dementia), the changes occurring are irreversible.

ALZHEIMER'S DISEASE: Alzheimer's disease is a progressive loss of mental ability and cognition, frequently accompanied by personality change and emotional instability. It is a common disease affecting both men and women; usually starting between ages 50 and 60, often with memory lapses, and changes in behavior; its progression to include symptoms of confusion, restlessness, inability to plan and carry out activities and sometimes hallucinations, delusional thinking, and loss of bladder control. The cause is medically unknown, but plaques and neurofibrillary tangles are commonly found in the brain tissues. There is no cure; the progression can be slowed by medication (Aricept, et al) with treatment aimed at alleviating the symptoms.

THE HOSPICE PHILOSOPHY

The majority of people want their loved to live as well as possible, even with an incurable disease. There comes a point, however, when aggressive treatment of the loved one's disease may compel them to decide that the burned exceeds the realistic benefit. This validates their freedom to choose the best quality of life possible, for whatever length of life.

When a patient's disease progresses to an incurable state, the medical modality of treatment changes from curative care, to palliative care. A range of treatments for symptoms may continue, including *chemotherapy, radiation, blood transfusions, paracentesis* (withdrawing fluid from the body), and *tube feeding*. These are all considered to be medical *comfort measures*; to achieve comfort care, and to relieve the pain. Thus, the medical model of treatment, *i.e.*, attempting to *treat and cure the disease*, moves to treating *the patient with a palliative modality*. That is, to provide comfort care, and to relieve pain, for as long as the patient has left to live.

The Hospice movement to avoid prolonging suffering from ineffective medical effort to conquer death, or from the opposite extreme, ignoring the dying, is not a modern concept. The culture of accepting the inevitable, in order to focus on easing the pathway from one phase of life to another, has deep roots extending back centuries, and even millennia, to periods when devoted spiritual leaders provided nurturing refuge to those in need, with the thought that God loves every person, and with the concept that Hospice Care is a worthwhile means for caregivers to return this love.

The ancient Hospice tradition has now been revived in the modern Hospice movement, in which, caring for the dying is not considered to be *a burden*, rather, *an opportunity* to provide comfort care with love, and provide a less difficult transition from this world to the next.

Revival of the modern Hospice concept came to fruition during the cultural turmoil of the 1960's, at which time Dr. Cicely Saunders pioneered and defined a hospice program in 1968 at St. Christopher's Hospital in London, England. The following year Dr. Elisabeth Kubler-Ross was a pioneer working with death and dying, and published a renowned work on *Death and Dying in America.*

The profound teachings and work of both Dr. Elisabeth Kubler-Ross, and Dr. Cicely Saunders throughout their active professional lives caused greater insight into both the pathway to death, and dying. Their work and concept is best expressed in the words of Dr. Cicely Saunders: *"The community needs the dying to make it think of eternal issues. We are indebted to those who can make us learn such things as to be gentle and to approach others with true affection and respect."* It appears as if she had returned full circle to the original concept of hospice that has existed in all cultures since the beginning of human life.

Today, the revived concept and practice of Hospice Care provides a new, holistic discipline and is a permanent part of modern life; it is an important response to ever-changing cultural conditions.

The distinct purpose of Hospice is to provide appropriate care and comfort, and a 24 Hour availability of professional care giver team members, who are sensitive to the patient's needs, enabling the patient to be remain in familiar surroundings, so as to better prepare the patient mentally, physically and spiritually for the major transition from this life to the next

THE HOSPICE CHAPLAIN

The Hospice Chaplain, also known as Spiritual Care Coordinator, is an equally important and integral part of the hospice team, providing compassionate care to people with terminal illness and their families.

The Chaplain's distinct education, skill, experience, and sense of calling, uniquely characterize the spiritual care professional. When patients and families require professional spiritual counsel and care, they turn to the hospice chaplain.

Some of the Chaplain's spiritual support services available for the patient and the families are: Increased understanding, acceptance and coping through prayer, reading from sacred texts, sacraments or other services as requested by patient or family Assistance with patient and family issues of meaninglessness, loss of faith, failure, anger, despair, betrayal, fear/dread, guilt, grief, hopelessness, forgiveness, bereavement, and general questions about the meaning of life and death. Assistance with connecting or re-connecting the patient and family With a place of worship or religious affiliation, and assist with Arrangements for a clergy to visit patient's home Assistance with funeral or memorial service arrangements and Information about religious practices

THE MISSION OF THE HOSPICE CHAPLAIN:

The profound mission of the Hospice Chaplain is succinctly encapsulated within two paragraphs in the forward to the *National Hospice and Palliative Care Organization* publication pamphlet under "Foundations of Spiritual Care in Hospice," page 2, which states, in part:

"The journey of dying provokes a heightened awareness of a person's morality, personal relationships and compelling spiritual issues. Dying is a profound rite of passage, sometimes mysterious and often filled with changes, suffering, distress and refining realizations for all involved. Concerned hospice professionals," ___ especially Chaplains ___ (author's comment) *"...are sojourners with patients in search for meaning, comfort, strength and hope. Practiced with reverence and compassion, in relationships of trust and mutuality, hospice care remains always essentially sacred and spiritual in nature.*

"Hospice brings to the end-of-life journey a holistic philosophy and practice intended to help patients and families accomplish with, dignity, the out-comes of self-determined life closure, safe and comfortable dying and effective grieving... Spiritual care in hospice supports the exercise of each person's unique spirituality, with the hope that meaning and love may be found in the presence of suffering and death.

THE GOAL OF THE HOPSICE CHAPLAIN: To assist the patient in having spiritual peace of mind, with the best quality of life possible, for whatever length of life they may have, and to die a peaceful death with dignity, in familiar surroundings, with family and friends present, to make the end-of-life experience as loving and comfortable as possible.

ABOUT THE AUTHOR

The Rev. Dr. Curtis E. Smith an ordained, non-denominational pastor has worked with terminally ill hospice patients for the past twenty three years. He holds graduate degrees in marriage and family counseling, religious education, and human behavior. He holds post-graduate degrees in psychology, religion and human behavior.

"Dr. Curtis," as he is fondly called by associates, colleagues, and patients, has extensive education and experience in both acute hospital care and hospice settings, with Brea Community Hospital, Brea, California, where he served for eight years as resident Staff Chaplain, and with Cancer Treatment Centers of America, who was at that time, also located in Brea Community Hospital. He currently works with Gentiva Health Care / Hospice Care, a national Health Care agency.

Dr. Curtis Smith is a published author and has written articles on death and dying, marriage, family, and religious articles dealing with life, spirituality and infinity. He has a Clinical Pastoral educational background having trained with a Clinical Pastoral Education training Center with the Crystal Cathedral located in Garden Grove, California.

For twenty plus years, Dr. Curtis Smith was in private practice working as a Clinical Pastoral Psychotherapist with a Clinical Psychologist colleague, Dr. M. David Riggs, and Dr. Glenn Balch, Licensed Marriage, Family and Child Counselor. At one time they operated five different offices located in Anaheim, Brea, Placentia, Yorba Linda, and Garden Grove, California. He resides with his family in Anaheim, California.

This work on Hospice, *Walking Through the Valley*, has been ten years in the writing; it is Dr. Smith's first, of four full length books. *Walking Through The Valley* is the Second Edition; the First Edition, was originally published under the title of *When It's Time*. The second edition has been updated and much additional material has been added.